R O B   C A R L E S S

CINQUE ANNI

THE STORY OF THE ITALIAN NATIONAL FOOTBALL TEAM

2 0 1 7 - 2 0 2 2

First published by Pitch Publishing, 2025

Pitch Publishing
9 Donnington Park,
85 Birdham Road,
Chichester, West Sussex,
PO20 7AJ
www.pitchpublishing.co.uk
info@pitchpublishing.co.uk

A CIP catalogue record is available for this book
from the British Library.

ISBN 978 1 83680 170 2

Typesetting and origination by Pitch Publishing

Printed and bound on FSC® certified paper in line with
our continuing commitment to ethical business practices,
sustainability and the environment.

Printed and bound in India by Thomson Press

Contents

To Erin – my first grandchild. My love for you knows no bounds.

To Claire – my love for you also knows no bounds.

x

Introduction

PERUGIA'S PRESIDENT, Luciano Gaucci, was not a happy man in the summer of 2002. There were a number of reasons for this. Firstly, he had just witnessed his beloved Italy being knocked out of the World Cup in the second round by South Korea. Secondly, the player who scored the winning goal played for his club.

Ahn Jung-Hwan had been plying his trade in Italy on loan since 2000 when he scored the winning 'golden goal' in the 117th minute of a pulsating match played in Daejeon in his home country. The elation of scoring that goal would have been juxtaposed the following day with the news that his contract in Italy was to be torn up. Gaucci offered no ambiguity as to why this was the case, proclaiming:

'That gentleman will never set foot in Perugia again. He was a phenomenon only when he played against Italy.

'I am a nationalist and I regard such behaviour not only as an affront to Italian pride but also an offence to a country which two years ago opened its doors to him. I have no intention of paying a salary to someone who has ruined Italian soccer.'

Given that this happened in the knockout stages of the World Cup finals, what would have been Luciano Gaucci's responses to those who knocked Italy out of the qualifying stages of the World Cup, preventing them from even reaching the finals?

Gaucci passed away on 1 February 2020. He had been alive to witness Italy's inability to qualify for the finals in Russia in 2018 – the first time that his country had failed to do so since 1958. What he missed after his passing were the prodigious extremes of consecutive failures to qualify to play on the world stage – as Italy didn't make it to Qatar 2022 either – while shining on the more local, European one.

Italy were not the first football superpower not to make its mark at consecutive World Cup finals. Perhaps the most significant absentee prior to the Italians were England, football's founding fathers who had failed to qualify for the 1974 finals held in West Germany and Argentina in 1978. Both of these tournaments saw Holland finish as runners-up in the final to their hosts. Therefore, Holland's failure to qualify in 1982 and 1986 also registered on the Richter scale – as did France in 1990 and 1994.

However, as rich as all these countries are in terms of prestige and heritage, they had all won just one major trophy each leading up to the 1998 finals: England winning the World Cup on home soil in 1966, and European Championship honours going to the French in 1984 and the Dutch four years later. By the time that Italy's sequential debacles had occurred, they had been crowned World Champions on four occasions and European winners as well.

One could argue the case for all of these nations when it comes to 12 years being a long time to be missing in World Cup action and they all would be salient.

Italy is different though. Very different. How so?

Well, firstly let us consider what they have achieved as a nation. They won the World Cup at the first time of asking in 1934. They won the European Championship the first time they actually qualified for the finals, so they are the most majestic of upstarts and debutants. They took to the stage and made the rest of the football world sit up and take notice: an orchestra of different sounds and notes perfected by an Italian conductor (Vittorio Pozzo) who changed everything in the 1930s. There was no 'difficult second album' in that decade for them either, as they retained their status as champions of the world in 1938.

However, they are a footballing nation of total extremes as well. Italian football knows nothing about middle ground. When it's good it's really good and when it's bad they go to pieces. Between 1950 and 1966, Italy failed to get out of the group stages in the World Cup finals and did not even qualify in 1958.

They are feast or famine. Beauty or the beast.

This makes them even more of an interest, an enigma that needs to be explored further.

This book details Italy's relationship with FIFA's World Cup and UEFA's European Championship, and the results that followed in each tournament under these banners. It is necessary and important to trace their pathway through these tournaments from the beginning, to illustrate how it all started for Italian football and where the rabbit holes took them, but it really does not get to the heart of why I was compelled to write this book.

How did a footballing nation that is congenial with greatness not qualify for not only ONE World Cup, but TWO?

Not only this, but that nation became European Champions in between and at a time when the world had basically shut down from a pandemic (Covid) that affected Italy more than most.

So, this is what sets the story apart from those other nations previously mentioned.

In football (as in life itself) success is not guaranteed. It is not a God-given right. It is something that needs to be earned. On that basis, no nation has the automatic right to bear arms in major tournaments, but I have spoken to friends and associates when out in social circles, and we have agreed that a tournament *sans Azzurri* is a poorer one. Why? The steel that encompassed the industry produced by Dino Zoff, Claudio Gentile and more recently, Giorgio Chiellini; then there is the sapphire production line, players such as Gianni Rivera, Roberto Baggio and Andrea Pirlo. There are many, many more. I can go back before those aforementioned and I can go forward with consummate ease. It is not an exclusive club, far from it and the rest of the book will seek them out; I merely wish to make my point about the greatness we have witnessed on the pitch over the decades and some of its components that make up the sum of all its parts.

Then there are the endearing images that have happened without the ball. One just needs to think about the goal celebration and the tears that flowed down the cheeks of Marco Tardelli in the World Cup Final of 1982. Then there was Salvatore Schillaci in unison with Roberto Baggio on home soil in 1990 – and there are more of these that occupy the mind's eye upon reflection.

Just how did all this happen to Italy? It has intrigued me greatly ever since the second coming of non-compliance for the World Cup held in Qatar in 2022.

There are many variables, and this book will set out to understand them.

The themes will cover scandal, stadiums, the demise of Serie A, tactics, succession planning, investment, club v country, finances, data and innovation, pivotal moments – all of them played a major part.

It has been previously stated that a World Cup without Italy is like pizza without cheese. Having not qualified for two consecutive competitions would suggest that there would be no sauce on the base either.

The hashtag *#Italiafuoridaimondiali* is translated to 'Italy is out of the World Cup' and it has been used more than 2,500 times since these failures. Now would be a perfect time for Italy to consign this to the dustbins of history, never to be repeated!

This is the story of how it all happened. *Forza Italia*!

Prologue

National Football Stadium, Windsor Park, Belfast
World Cup Qualification Group C
15 November 2021

The football faithful of Northern Ireland's national
team on home soil had not been used to the art of goal
celebration during the 2022 World Cup qualifying
campaign. In fact, prior to the last game, the chance
to jump out of their seats, punch the air and hug the
like-minded, green-and-white attired people on either
side of them, had been most rare to say the least. (Solace
could be regained though, as there had been no similar
happenings in the away end either.) Northern Ireland had
had a goal to celebrate just once before in the campaign,

and that had been just three days earlier, when they had hosted the country that had occupied the bottom place in Group C throughout – Lithuania. To make things even more egregious, it was not even a Northern Ireland player whose goal divided the two countries – it was an own goal by Lithuania's centre-back, Benas Šatkus, in the 17th minute, which settled matters.

Now they were down to their final game of the campaign, and they could not mathematically qualify for Qatar – that ship had sailed several games before. They were playing a country that could still qualify – a country that sat top of the group. Italy. As the Irish folk from the north of the country took their seats prior to this game, they would not have expected to buck the goal-scoring trend that they had accustomed themselves to. In fact, they were expecting to be well beaten by a country that had graced so many previous World Cup qualifying campaigns – and indeed had won the finals four times.

Genesis

THE ORIGINS of football in Italy date back many centuries, just as they do for many other countries, and they are inextricably linked by the same trope. A 'ball' was used on a 'piece of land' by a group of people; the land varied in size, while the game varied in structure and execution. One of the earliest forms occurred in the Roman Empire and was known as '*Harpastum*'. The game involved balls that were stuffed with feathers. They were not as big as the footballs we see today. Little is known about the actual dimensions, but the likelihood is that it was more 'softball' than anything else. Due to the expansion of the Empire, it became a very popular sport. Derived from a Greek game called '*Phaininda*' or '*Episkyros*', matters on the pitch were decided by retaining the ball for as long as possible and by using varying degrees of speed, agility and physical exertion. The physical side was most prominent and was prone to acts of violence, with limbs broken at regular intervals.

Further adaptions to the game were made in the 16th century in Florence, the capital city of Tuscany in central Italy. Known as '*Calcio Storico Fiorentino*' during the renaissance period, it was mainly played by the upper classes and the rich and famous. It wasn't just played in Florence, though, as there are reports that the game was even played by various Popes in the Vatican City. It was similar to the ancient times in as much as it could get very violent, but the *raison d'être* was to score more goals than the opponents. The term *'calcio'* means 'kick' and is still used today as the name for association football in Italy.

Association football was started in England in 1863 and the opening of the Suez Canal just six years later created the chance for English communities to stop off on new routes between their home ports and India. Italy was an important part of the route, and whilst in port, sailors would gather for 'kick-abouts'. This happened at several ports in the region, including Naples, Genoa, Livorno and Palermo, and locals were invited to make up the numbers. The popularity of the more modern adaption of the game had started to increase, especially on the docksides. This gave way for people to take the game further inland and to the masses.

The pioneer of this was a man called Edoardo Bosio. Born in Turin in 1864, Bosio spent a great deal of time in the United Kingdom (mainly in the textile industry) where many football clubs turned professional and the Football Association – the first of its kind – was born. Bosio very much liked what he was witnessing and wanted to set up something similar in his native country. Upon returning to Turin in 1887, Bosio set about forming Italy's first football team – the Torino Football and Cricket Club –

which was made up mainly of his co-workers in the textile business. However, Bosio faced two issues. Firstly, there were no rules to abide by, so it was very much a kick-about still, in the style that had been played in the ports. Also, there were no other teams to play against, but this would soon change in and around the Turin region. Football was still very much a 'local' sport, and there were no official teams. However, in September 1893, the Genoa Cricket and Football Club was formed by the British Consulate. It was not an inclusive project to start off with as Italians were not allowed to be members. In 1894, another club was formed in Turin, Football Club Torinese. Again, the rules were open to interpretation and teams seldom travelled so the matches were local affairs.

This would change just three years later thanks to the game's second pioneer.

James Richardson Spensley was born in London in 1867. He was a doctor and had arrived in Genoa in 1896, initially to treat sailors from the coal ships. A much-travelled man, Richardson Spensley found himself managing the football side for Genoa soon after. One of the first things that he did was to negotiate with the British Consulate to allow Italians to be members of the club for the first time. As well as taking an authoritarian role within the club, he could also play the game and his favoured positions were goalkeeper or defender.

It would not be long before the first official match in Italy was played between his team and Football Club Torinese, on 6 January 1898, with the first official championship taking place on 8 May 1898 in Turin under the guidance of the Italian Football Federation. It was known as *Campionato Italiano di Football* and would feature teams in the northern region of the country. There were just three matches played, all on the same day. In the morning, Internazionale FC Torino beat FBC Torinese, and RS Ginnastica Torino lost to Genoa, then in the final match later in the day, Genoa beat Internazionale FC Torino 2-1 after extra time and thus became the first champions of Italian football.

Such was Genoa's dominance in the early years of Italian club football, they were crowned champions a further five times in the next six years, only not winning in 1901 when AC Milan claimed their first championship.

During their last season of dominance, in 1904, there was a change of name for the competition as it became the Prima Categoria, and it was during this period that national sentiments came to the fore that would ultimately give rise to the national team.

In 1907, the competition was split into two areas.

The Italian Championship was deemed to be the most important as only Italian players were allowed to participate. The victors would be crowned *Campioni d'Italia* (Italian Champions) and would be awarded the Coppa Buni.

The Federal Championship was deemed to be a secondary competition where foreign players were allowed to play. The only caveat (apart from ability) was that they had to reside in Italy. In this competition, the victors would be crowned *Campioni Federali* (Federal Champions) and would be awarded the Coppa Spensley.

The rationale for the two championships was to ultimately strengthen the national cause as it allowed the weaker clubs to win trophies and develop winning mentalities.

The majority of big clubs (Genoa, Torino and Milan) withdrew from both championships in order to protest against the autocratic policies that were being set up by the powers that be, and it wasn't until the 1909/10 season that the format was changed to nine teams playing each other home and away, representing the introduction of a league that it is now known as Serie A and Serie B. There were more changes to the name (Prima Divisione and Divisione Nazionale) and format over the years, with northern and southern regions being introduced before amalgamation.

Club football had grown in popularity, importance and influence. And it wasn't just on the pitch that this was happening, but moreover within the walls of Italian politics, the union between the two forming at a very early stage and, in reality, the game has been held in ligature ever since.

With the rules initially put into place by James Richardson Spensley and the changes enforced under Prima Categoria, it invariably led to interest in a national team to represent Italy on the world stage. There had been an attempt to set this up at the end of the 19th century when an Italian select team played against a side from Switzerland. The game was played, unsurprisingly, in Turin on 30 April 1899. Little is known about it, other than it was the Swiss who travelled back home the happier after picking up a 2-0 away victory.

History was made on 15 May 1910 when Italy played their first official (FIFA-recognised) international match, hosting France at Civico Arena, Milan. The crowd was estimated to be 4,000. The referee was an Englishman called Henry Goodley. The team wore white as no official colours had been agreed at this stage. This would soon change though, with blue being chosen to honour the Italian house of Savoy, the country's royal family since unification in 1861. The Italian side was picked by a committee (as was the general case in football at that time) that consisted of Umberto Meazza, Agostino Recalcati, Alberto Crivelli, Giannino Camperio and Giuseppe Gamba. The captain for the historic first match was Francesco Calì.

The match sprung to life in the 13th minute when AC Milan's Pietro Lana gave Italy the lead, therefore having the honour of being his country's first ever goalscorer. The lead was doubled just seven minutes later when Virgilio Fossati converted. A few minutes into the second half Henri Bellocq reduced the deficit, but the first ever goal conceded by Italy didn't rattle them and soon after it was 3-1 when Lana scored his second goal of the match. Once more, the French came roaring back, and the deficit was reduced to just one when Jean Ducret scored in the

62nd minute. The Italians were still not fazed by this, and it was 4-2 just moments later, Giuseppe Rizzi on the scoresheet. That would signal the end of the French resistance as two further goals in the last ten minutes signalled a famous Italian win. The fifth goal was scored by Rizzi before Lana capped a wonderful match with his third from the penalty spot, to make the final score Italy 6 France 2.

The starting line-up that represented Italy in their first ever official international match was made up of players that primarily played for US Milanese, Andrea Dona, Torino, AC Milan, Inter Milan and Ausonia. The system that was played in the match was 2-3-5 – also known as 'the pyramid of Cambridge'. The apex of the formation was the goalkeeper and it was very much an inverted system that was invented in England and used for several decades, firstly in the country of its origin and then picked up by the rest of the world.

Italy's first match on the international stage had exceeded all expectations. Such was the gratitude from the Italian fans that they rewarded the players with packets of cigarettes. Confidence was now sky high, but this was reined in during the course of Italy's second foray. Just 11 days later, on 26 May 1910, Italy were soundly beaten by the Hungarian national team at the Millenáris Sporttelep in Budapest. With 15 minutes remaining, Hungary had raced into a 6-0 lead, leaving the Italians somewhat sundered. Even though Giuseppe Rizzi pulled a goal back in the 88th minute, it really was just a consolation calling card, as the match finished 6-1 in favour of the hosts.

There would be no further matches in the calendar year, but Italy would have the chance to exact early revenge in 1911 when they hosted Hungary on 6 January. The match was played at the Arena Civica in Milan. Once more, the eastern European country came out on top, albeit in a much closer fashion, with Hungary winning the match by a single goal scored by Imre Schlosser in the 22nd minute.

Three other friendlies were played in the same year, the first being against France away in Saint-Ouen. This time it would be up to the French to try to provide the dish best served cold. However, the Italians were resolute and put up a much better fight than they had done in Budapest the year before. The match finished all-square with the two countries sharing four goals, with Carlo Rampini and Arturo Boiocchi replying either side of goals scored by Eugène Maës. Italy then played two matches against Switzerland, who they had played in their first unofficial match in 1899. Once again, the Swiss came out on top after the two matches, although the Italians could seek solace in the fact that this time the game on home soil did not end in defeat, after another 2-2 draw in Milan. The scorers were Gustavo Carrer and Boiocchi, who had now scored in two consecutive matches. It was not to be three on the trot though as Switzerland ran out 3-0 winners in the city of La Chaux-de-Fonds.

There would be a further five matches played in 1912, resulting in losses in international friendlies to both

France and Austria. First came a 4-3 defeat to the French on 17 March, followed by a 3-1 reverse against Austria in December. Both losses were on Italian soil. The other games were part of the 1912 Summer Olympics held in Sweden. Once more, Italy would taste defeat in the first round against Finland, losing the match 3-2 after extra time. They then played two other matches as a first-round defeat meant games in the 'consolation tournament'. Italy defeated the hosts 1-0 thanks to a goal scored by Franco Bontadini, but then fell foul of a rampant Austria team, losing the match 5-1.

Italy also played an exhibition match in 1912, against an English team called English Wanderers, with the match ending 1-1. Fixtures like this were unofficial, as they were not recognised by FIFA. The next match of this kind came against Reading FC on 18 May 1913. It was played in Turin, with the English team winning 2-0. In total, Italy have played 27 matches that have been classed as unofficial, with the last one being played against a select team from Cagliari at the time of writing this book (August 2024). The national team won 12-0 in Sardinia, with the game only lasting for 60 minutes.

In terms of results, 1913 was not a vintage year for the Azzurri – they played only three games, losing two and winning just one, with the solitary win coming against Belgium with a goal scored by Guido Ara in the 57th minute. It would be the only time that the team would celebrate a goal in 1913 as they lost 1-0 to France and 2-0 against Austria. However, there would be a marked improvement in results in 1914, when they remained undefeated after four matches, recording two wins and two draws. The wins came against France, 2-0, in Milan and their first ever victory on foreign soil (save for the Olympics) with a 1-0 win against Switzerland, Luigi Barbesino scoring the only goal. The draws came against Austria and the Swiss.

The unbeaten run continued into the early days of 1915 when Italy once again defeated Switzerland in Turin, on 31 January. It was a real family affair with Aldo Cevenini scoring two of the goals alongside his older brother, Luigi, who scored the other. This would be the last official game played by Italy until 1920, because of the First World War. A further six unofficial games were contested between 1915 and 1919, however, the last three being played as part of the Inter-Allied Games in Paris after the Allied victory in the war. The group stages saw the Italians paired with Greece, Romania and France. It was a complete goal fest in the first two games with Italy beating Greece 9-0 and Romania 7-1. The only defeat occurred in the final group game, where France won 2-0. Despite the heroics in the first two matches, Italy didn't progress any further in the tournament.

There was an explosive start in Italy's first official game after the war, in 1920. Another friendly against France was played on 18 January in Milan and the 14,000 in the Velodromo Sempione were treated to a game that had 13 goals, with nine of them being celebrated by the home nation. Aldo Cevenini opened the scoring in the seventh minute and by the time the referee had blown for half-time, there had been another six goals. Cevenini added his second on 18 minutes just before Ermanno Aebi extended the lead further. France then cut the deficit by scoring a couple of goals themselves before the half-hour mark via Paul Nicolas and Henri Bard. Moments later the lead was extended when Guglielmo Brezzi put the ball into the net. A frantic first half of goals was completed by Bard just before half-time for his second (and his country's third) goal of a pulsating match. The Italians were even more of a threat in the second half and by the 84th minute, they had scored a further five goals with Aebi and Brezzi both netting twice to complete their hat-tricks. The other goal for the home nation was converted by Carlo Carcano. France did manage to score a fourth in the dying minutes through Raymond Dubly, but it was all in vain as the Italians won 9-4.

Italy participated in the Summer Olympics in 1920, in Belgium, and they made a winning start in a game which made history, as it was against the first non-European country that they had played against. The 2-1 victory over Egypt occurred on 28 August with goals from Adolfo Baloncieri and Guglielmo Brezzi. This win put the Italians into the quarter-finals, and they would face their old adversaries, France, the day after the win against the African nation. France won the match, 3-1. Italy would then once more play in the consolation tournament, where they beat Norway 2-1 after extra time to set up their first ever encounter with Spain. And it was the Spanish celebrating, with a 2-0 victory to end Italy's football interest in the tournament until 1924.

The next Olympics was held in France and Italy would once again reach the quarter-finals. The difference from four years previous was that it took them a further round to get there. A 1-0 victory over Spain was followed up with a 2-0 win against Luxembourg in Paris. Any medal hopes were dashed when Switzerland beat them 2-1, once again in the capital. There were no consolation matches this time.

Just prior to the Paris tournament, Italy had been soundly beaten by Hungary, 7-1, with the unwanted record of it being their heaviest defeat. There was better news for Italy the following year as they recorded their biggest win to date with a 7-0 home victory against France. Leopoldo Conti opened the account after just four minutes and that was the only goal scored in the first half, the blitz occurring in the second period with braces from Adolfo Baloncieri, Virgilio Levratto and Giovanni Moscardini completing the rout.

The rest of the decade was made up of friendly internationals, and a couple more unofficial matches. The results (like they had been in the previous ten years) were mixed. However, in a newly formed competition from 1927, and at the 1928 Summer Olympics, the football world started to take more notice of Italy.

The first Central European International Cup was played between 18 September 1927 and 11 May 1930. The tournament's structure was a round-robin competition for the five teams involved: Italy, Austria, Czechoslovakia, Hungary and Switzerland. The tournament was later known as the Antonín Švehla Cup in honour of the Czechoslovakian prime minister of the same name, who would present the winners with a Bohemian crystal cup. The trophy went to Italy, who finished top of the group with 11 points (one more than Austria and Czechoslovakia). It was a tight tournament, with Hungary on nine points themselves, but the exception was Switzerland who suffered eight consecutive defeats. Italy's record was played eight matches, won five, drawn one and lost two. There were 86 goals scored in 20 matches, for an average of 4.3 goals per match. Italy were the highest scorers with 21 goals and two of their players were leading goalscorers alongside Hungary's Ferenc Hirzer on six goals. These were Gino Rossetti and Julio Libonatti.

There was further progress made in the Summer Olympics held in the Netherlands with the Italians claiming a bronze medal. The first-round match took place on 29 May and a seven-goal thriller was served up against France in Amsterdam, with Italy winning 4-3. The reward was a quarter-final against Spain which eventually went to a replay after the teams drew 1-1. In the replay the Italians once again found their scoring boots with an emphatic 7-1 victory. Dreams of standing on the gold podium were dashed when they played their first ever match against South American opposition in the form of Uruguay. The scoreline was 3-2 in favour of the South Americans. Italy then played Egypt once more for the right to claim the bronze medal and they completed the task in some style. The match started at a blistering pace and the half-time score was 6-2 to Italy. If the players and fans thought the second half would be a much more sombre affair, where breaths could be taken, then they were seriously wrong, as Italy scored five more and Egypt just one, the match finishing 11-3 to Italy. Three players recorded hat-tricks in the game: Angelo Schiavio, Elvio Banchero and Mario Magnozzi. The other two goals were scored by Adolfo Baloncieri.

For the vast majority of their first 20 years in international football existence, Italy had been managed by committee, with coaches being put in charge at various times. The coaches were Umberto Meazza, William Garbutt and Vincenzo Resegotti. The exceptions occurred mainly in the latter years of the 1920s. Augusto Rangone was the manager who oversaw the start of the Central European International Cup campaign, and the bronze medal in the Olympics. He was followed by Carlo Carcano, an ex-international player for Italy who only lasted just over six months in the job.

What Italy required was someone who could build on the successes afforded to the nation just as the 1930s were about to commence; a man who could take the position and maintain the winning philosophy. That man was Vittorio Pozzo. He wasn't exactly new to the role when he took up the position as manager of the national team on 1 December 1929. Like Rangone, Pozzo had served on the committee and taken up the position of head coach on a temporary basis on two separate occasions – firstly in 1912 and then for a brief spell in 1924. His record wasn't something that had pulled up any Italian trees during this time, taking charge of just eight games, winning only three. All this was about to change, though.

The 1920s had not been roaring for the Azzurri. But the impending 1930s certainly would be as Italy aimed for world domination, in a brand-new competition that was about to start and that would change international football forever.

And they did it not once, but twice as well!

Italy and the World Cup: 1930–2014

THE WORLD'S governing body of football was founded in 1904 in Paris and was known as *Fédération Internationale de Football Association*, or the International Federation of Association Football, in English, and was abbreviated to FIFA. It was originally designed to oversee international affairs for a select number of countries – Belgium, Denmark, France, Germany, Holland, Spain, Sweden and Switzerland. Whilst there had been an 'unofficial World Cup' tournament between 1909 and 1911 (known as the Lipton Trophy, it was backed by the Lipton Tea company and the Italian royal family and was more about club football), the most prestigious international tournament in the early part of the 20th century had been the Summer Olympics. However, as the 1920s progressed, football was becoming more professional and setting up a World Cup was deemed to be a necessity, and thus the first tournament was organised, to be played in 1930.

Italy originally put in a bid to host the competition, but withdrew their application alongside Sweden,

Holland and Spain. This left Uruguay with a clear run to become the first hosts. Participation take-up was very slow, especially among the European countries. There were many reasons for this. Firstly, economic downturns, with the costs associated with travel being too much to bear. Also, many players were not willing to be away from their families for the period of time it would take for the tournament to take place. Denmark and Germany refused to take part as they considered the professional aspects of the game to be negative. England refused to participate as the competition was not seen as 'prestigious' enough.

All-in-all, there were 13 countries that contested the inaugural World Cup, which ran from 13 to 30 July. They were Argentina, Belgium, Brazil, Bolivia, Chile, France, Mexico, Paraguay, Peru, Romania, United States, Uruguay and Yugoslavia. Three other countries should have taken part: Egypt missed the boat and Japan and Siam withdrew.

The format was group, semi-final and the final itself, at the Estadio Centenario in Montevideo, in front of 80,000 people. Uruguay became the champions, beating Argentina 4-2 in the final.

The World Cup was now up and running.

1934 World Cup
Manager: Vittorio Pozzo

Italy may have withdrawn from hosting the event in 1930 but they were successful in 1934 when they were awarded the competition that took place between 27 May and 10

June. There were changes made to the format, as it was now open to qualification with 32 counties competing in order to reach the finals that would see 16 teams participate in Italy. Despite being the hosts, Italy still had to play their qualifying match, and this took place on 25 March 1934 as they entertained Greece in Milan. The qualification process was marred by teams withdrawing either before or during this phase. This meant that there were only two teams vying for qualification from Group 3 and only one game took place. It was a resounding win for the Italians, as they took the Greeks apart to win the match 4-0, Giuseppe Meazza netting a goal in each half, with the others scored by Anfilogino Guarisi and Giovanni Ferrari.

There was one notable absentee from the qualification and the finals, and that was the defending champions, Uruguay. This was because they had decided to boycott the World Cup in Europe, due to the lack of teams that had participated just four years previously.

The group stage that had been in operation at the first World Cup was discarded in favour of a straight knockout tournament. If a match was tied after 90 minutes, then an extra 30 minutes were played. If the score was still tied after extra time, the match would be replayed the next day, so there were no penalty shoot-outs.

The 15 countries that played in the finals, alongside Italy, were Argentina, Austria, Belgium, Brazil, Czechoslovakia, Egypt, France, Germany, Hungary, Netherlands, Romania, Spain, Sweden, Switzerland and the United States. Eight stadiums were used during the tournament, located in Milan, Bologna, Rome, Florence, Naples, Genoa, Turin and Trieste (located at the head of the Gulf of Trieste, on a narrow strip of Italian territory lying between the Adriatic Sea and Slovenia). All eight first round matches kicked off at the same time and Italy's marker was dug deep into the ground with an outstanding display against the United States that saw them win 7-1 in Rome. Angelo Schiavio created history by being the first Italian to score three times in a single World Cup match. Raimundo Orsi scored two and the other goals were from Giovanni Ferrari and Giuseppe Meazza. There could have been a few more goals for the team in blue if it had not been for the US goalkeeper Julius Hjulian.

The quarter-finals paired Italy against Spain in Florence on 31 May (four days after the first matches). History was once more made as the match finished 1-1 and became the first game in the World Cup finals to be replayed. Luis Regueiro had given the Spaniards the lead on the half-hour mark before Giovanni Ferrari equalised a minute before the break. The replay also took place in Florence and only one goal separated the two countries, Giuseppe Meazza scoring in the 11th minute of the match.

Italy then faced Austria in the semi-finals played at the San Siro in Milan on 3 June. It was once more a tight affair with only one goal, scored by Enrique Guaita (who also represented Argentina).

The stage was set for the second World Cup Final which took place on 10 June 1934 in Rome with Italy taking on Czechoslovakia, in front of a crowd of 55,000. The Czechs had made it to the final by beating Romania, Switzerland and Germany. In keeping with Italy's last three matches, the final was a very close affair, which went into extra time.

Czechoslovakia took the lead when Antonín Puč scored in the 71st minute. Ten minutes later and parity had been restored, Raimundo Orsi netting. The winning goal came just five minutes into extra time when Angelo Schiavio secured himself a place in national folklore, giving the Italians their world title at the first time of asking. Vittorio Pozzo had created magic and it would not be the last time in the decade either.

The final had been played at the Stadio Nazionale PNF, the stadium of the National Fascist Party, and before the finals were played, Italian politics once more embedded itself firmly into Italian sport. The prime minister was Benito Mussolini. His detractors accused him of using the tournament to promote his fascist regime and to curry favour for Italy by means of corruption and meddling. Whether this was the case or not remains open to debate, but Italy's manager in terms of football was soon to prove that his team could also hit the heights away from Italian soil, and on a number of fronts.

Their very first match after being crowned World Champions ended in defeat, but it was the first time Italy had met the country that had given them so much inspiration at the end of the 19th century – England. The match took place in London at Highbury, the home of Arsenal FC, on 14 November 1934. England took the game to the Italians from kick-off and were three goals to the good after just 12 minutes, with Eric Brook opening the scoring after three minutes and extending the lead seven minutes later, having also missed a first-minute penalty. To make matters worse for Italy, Arsenal legend Ted Drake made it three shortly after. Italy were rocked but managed to pick themselves up in the second half to make the scoreline a more respectable 3-2, Giuseppe Meazza scoring both goals.

Prior to the match, Mussolini had offered the players an Alfa Romeo car each and exemptions from any military service if they won. The match had been dubbed 'the real World Cup' in some quarters, with it seemingly meaning more to the pupils of the game, Italy. They were certainly keen to take on the nation that had inspired them to take up the game and actually win.

The match became known as the 'Battle of Highbury'. Tensions boiled over very early in the game, after England's Ted Drake had gone into a tackle with Italian centre-half, Luis Monti, with the upshot being a broken foot for the Italian defender. Monti stayed on the pitch for another ten minutes or so (there were no substitutes in internationals at the time). He could barely walk and it was during that time that England were able to stretch their lead. This incident (as well as the feeling that England were not taking the game seriously and therefore showing the visitors no respect) infuriated Monti's team-mates, ensuring a first-half bloodbath with broken noses, and black eyes amongst other injuries.

Italy won their final game of a superb year, however, beating Hungary 4-2 in Milan on 9 December.

1935 saw the World Champions mostly play the last remaining games of the 1933–35 Central European International Cup. They had been runners-up in the 1931–32 tournament, after winning the inaugural one in the decade before, but were back to winning ways once more as they topped the group on 11 points (two more than Austria and Hungary, who finished second and third respectively).

There was also joy in the 1936 Summer Olympics as Italy claimed the gold medal. The tournament was held in Berlin and the final took place on 15 August when Italy beat Austria 2-1 after extra time, Annibale Frossi scoring both goals. The Italians had seen off challenges from USA (1-0) and Japan (8-0), then beaten Norway in the semi-finals. Just like the final itself, that match went to extra time, where the Azzurri won 2-1. Frossi was once more the hero with the winning goal.

1938

Manager: Vittorio Pozzo

The 1938 World Cup was held in France and as defending champions, Italy did not have to qualify this time around. The year before had seen them compete in friendlies and the 1936–38 Central European International Cup.

However, the fourth instalment of the competition was not completed due to the annexation of Austria to Nazi Germany. Only Switzerland were able to fulfil all their fixtures, with Italy only playing four out of the eight, remaining in second place behind Hungary.

Italy's first match of the World Cup was a repeat of the semi-final victory over Norway in the 1936 Summer Olympics, in terms of opponents and a 2-1 win after extra time. Instead of Berlin, this match was played in Marseille on 5 June. The champions were up and running as early as the second minute with Pietro Ferraris opening proceedings. Just like the previous match, it was a very tight affair which was compounded in the 83rd minute when Norway equalised through Arne Brustad. The winning strike came early in the first period of extra time when Norwegian hearts where once more broken by the Italians as Silvio Piola netted.

The quarter-finals paired Italy against France in Paris a week after their first match. Gino Colaussi gave the Italians the lead after just nine minutes, but this was cancelled out a minute later when France equalised via Oscar Heisserer, who sent the vast majority of the crowd of just under 59,000 wild in celebration. However, by the end of the match, it was the Italian fans who were celebrating, as two second-half goals converted by Piola gave Italy a famous 3-1 victory to send the hosts out.

The semi-final showdown with Brazil took place on 16 June in Marseille, where they had beaten Norway, and again Italy won the match 2-1. This time, though, there was no need for extra time. There had been no goals in the first half but the game really came alight in the 51st minute when Gino Colaussi gave the Italians the lead, which was then doubled on the hour mark when Giuseppe Meazza converted a penalty. Brazil made it a nervous last few minutes when Romeu Pellicciari halved the deficit, but the blue wall could not be torn down, and Italy were in their second consecutive World Cup Final.

This time their opponents were Hungary, who had knocked out Dutch East Indies (Indonesia – the first Asian team to reach the finals), Switzerland and Sweden. The final was played on 19 June in Paris, attended by a crowd of 45,000. The game would once more see both teams coming out and making a quick impression. Italy drew first blood by taking the lead in the sixth minute through Gino Colaussi. The lead lasted just two minutes as Pál Titkos restored parity for the Hungarians. Italy were not to be denied though and scored two more first-half goals, through Silvio Piola (his fourth of the competition) and a second for Colaussi. With the score 3-1 at the break, the champions were in control, but Hungary continued to make a game of it and were rewarded in the 70th minute when György Sárosi made it 3-2. Italian nerves were settled in the 82nd minute when Piola scored.

Before the finals, Benito Mussolini had sent the team a telegram, which, according to urban legend, contained little in terms of words but was large in its sentiment. It (allegedly) read: *'Vincere o morire!'* – 'Win or die!'

However, this was later refuted by Italian player Pietro Rava: 'No, no, no, that's not true. He sent a telegram wishing us well, but never "win or die".'

There is no official record of the telegram, but it is fair to say that regardless of whether it did exist or not, Italy had chosen to win.

Italy had successfully defended the World Cup and Vittorio Pozzo had guided Italy into the 1930s and made them World Champions at the first and second times of asking as well as Olympic champions and twice winners of the Central European International Cup. It had been a wonderful achievement that had gone beyond the wildest of Italian dreams.

Pozzo had revolutionised the game by introducing a new method of play and also bringing unity to the national team in tournaments. The new tactic was known as the *Metodo* system. One of the main ideas was to have two defenders, known as 'full-backs', pushed out into wider positions, alongside the more recognised central defence pairing. This created the need for a more central midfield player to operate in between them, not only breaking up play but also being creative, supporting not just the defence, but moreover, the rest of the advanced midfield and attack. Therefore, this was the introduction of the 'playmaker'. The *Metodo* system was invented to allow highly technical teams to prosper by being able to slow down play and retain possession with shorter passing methods and it was based on a 2-3-2-3 system, a tactic that had served Italy so well during this golden period.

Pozzo would introduce training camps prior to the major tournaments, allowing more time for his teams to gel with preparation being the key component. He was also able to take advantage of picking players that had Italian ancestry, i.e., foreign-born Italian nationals. One of the most successful imports was Raimundo Orsi. The quick-footed left-winger had played for his native Argentina in the 1920s before moving to Italy in 1929, where he would go on to have a spectacular career mainly for Juventus and the national side. This use of foreign-born players was known in Italy as *'Oriundo'* and had its fair share of criticism. Upon hearing of this, Pozzo famously replied, 'If they can die for Italy, they can also play for Italy,' referring to the fact that such players had also served in the Italian army.

Vittorio Pozzo's standing in the pantheon of Italian footballing legends will never be diminished: a light that will never go out.

* * *

Due to the outbreak of World War Two, the World Cup was not played in either 1942 or 1946, so it would be a further 12 years before Italy could defend the title that they had practically made their own. By then, they would have new management at the helm as Pozzo resigned in 1948 after losing to England.

Perhaps it was felt that due to the major successes under Pozzo, it would be almost an impossibility to replace the man who had transformed Italian football, so Italy went back into the hands of a technical committee, led by Ferruccio Novo alongside Aldo Bardelli, Roberto Copernico and Vincenzo Biancone, for the next World Cup, held in Brazil.

1950

Host nation Brazil had requested certain changes to the format of the 1950 World Cup finals to maximise all commercial aspects due to the costly infrastructure put in place, and this was granted. Uruguay won the competition by topping the final group matches with the last game, which was played against Brazil with them winning 2–1. It would also be the first time that England had participated and they were made immediate favourites for the tournament.

There may have been a new format but some of the old issues once again occurred, with countries pulling out of the competition, citing the financial aspects of travel. Most noticeable was France's decision to do this. Therefore only 13 countries took part. Italy were placed in Group 3 alongside Sweden and Paraguay. The group had included India before they withdrew. Much to the surprise of the football world, Italy were knocked out before they had played their second game in the tournament.

The first game in Group 3 took place at the Pacaembu Stadium in São Paulo on 25 June 1950, with Italy playing

Sweden in front of a crowd of 36,502. As they had done in the 1938 finals, Italy came out of the proverbial traps the fastest and raced into the lead after just seven minutes, with Riccardo Carapellese putting them 1-0 up. This lead lasted until Sweden equalised courtesy of a goal from Hasse Jeppson. The favourites to qualify from the group were once more rocked just a few minutes later when Sweden took the lead through Sune Andersson. Sweden extended this lead further with 22 minutes remaining of the second half when Jeppson scored his second goal of the match. Ermes Muccinelli pulled a goal back with 15 minutes remaining, but the defending champions could not score again, with Sweden winning the match 3-2.

This meant that Italy's next match against Paraguay was a must-win – and win was exactly what the Azzurri did, beating the South American team 2-0 at the same stadium where they had played Sweden. Carapellese once more opened the scoring, with Egisto Pandolfini grabbing the second. The problem was that Italy had already been knocked out by the time this match took place on 2 July. A 2-2 draw between Sweden and Paraguay in Curitiba, just three days before, had ensured that Italy's participation in the tournament would go no further, because Sweden were uncatchable at the top of the group. Upon completing the second game, the committee that had taken over from Pozzo parted company with the national team.

To the rest of the football world, it may have been a shock to witness this early elimination, but this was not the case in Italy itself. On 4 May 1949, a plane carrying the Grande Torino side which had won every Italian league title since the end of World War Two, crashed into the basilica of Superga, which lay atop a hill on the outskirts of Turin. The crash took the lives of all who were aboard, with 31 souls perishing. The team was that good that the vast majority of it would have gone to the 1950 World Cup and heralded a new dawn in Italian national football. Understandably the crash took its toll on not only football, but the country itself.

The tragedy occurred on a return flight from Lisbon in Portugal. The plane had touched down in Barcelona to refuel. During the stopover, the club had lunch with AC Milan delegates, before embarking on their final flight to Turin. The flightpath headed south over mountains, and it was here that the weather turned, with strong winds and heavy cloud cover that reached perilously close to ground level, resulting in the plane being pushed off course as it made its final journey towards the runway.

The World Cup preparation that had been key for Italy in 1934 and 1938 was severely impacted in 1950 by depleted talent and travel. Italy reached Brazil by sea and not air, a route which took far longer, as the newly formed team sailed across the Atlantic with many players experiencing seasickness. In the end, it was Uruguay who once more lifted the trophy as they had done in 1930, beating Brazil 2-1 in the decisive game, and equalling Italy's record.

Albert Einstein had once decreed that 'adversity introduces a man to himself' and the initial years after the 1950 World Cup brought a wave of optimism as Italian football sought to rise once more from the tragedy that had befallen it in 1949. The national team lost only two matches in 1951–52, the highlight being an 8-0 victory over the USA in the preliminary round of the 1952 Summer Olympics held in Finland. The Italians were knocked out in the first round though, losing 3-0 to Hungary, a result which was repeated in Rome a year later in the 1948–53 Central European International Cup, Italy eventually finishing in fourth place.

In qualification for the 1954 World Cup, Italy were placed in Group 9 and their only opponents were Egypt, who they met on a home and away basis. The first match took place on 13 November 1953 at the Mokhtar El Tetsh Stadium in Cairo. It looked ominous for the visitors when Ad-Diba opened the scoring for the hosts just after the half-hour mark, but two goals in the second half scored by Amleto Frignani and Ermes Muccinelli gave Italy a 2-1 win, putting them in pole position for the return leg which was played on 24 January 1954. Muccinelli extended Italy's aggregate lead to two goals in the first minute of the match at the San Siro in Milan. Egypt got a goal back on 32 minutes through Alaa El-Hamouly. However, four more Italian goals in the second half put paid to the African nation's hopes of progressing, making the final score 5-1 on the night and 7-2 on aggregate to the Italians, with Frignani, Eduardo Ricagni and a brace from Giampiero Boniperti inflicting the damage. Italy would be playing in their fourth consecutive World Cup finals, which were to be held in Switzerland from 16 June to 4 July.

1954

Once more, the 1954 tournament had changes made to the format. Groups were still used but this time there would be seedings amongst the 16 countries that qualified. Each group contained two seeded and two non-seeded teams and no matches would take place between the two seeded or indeed the non-seeded teams. The other main difference was that if matches were drawn after 90 minutes, then extra time would be required, and only if the teams were level at that point would the game be classed as a draw.

Italy were once more under the management of a new technical committee, consisting of Lajos Czeizler, Angelo Schiavio and the coach, Silvio Piola, who had served the nation so well as a player. Italy were drawn in the same group (4) as England, the hosts and Belgium. Italy and England were the seeded teams and as a result would not play each other.

Italy's opening match took place on 17 June against Switzerland at the Stade Olympique de la Pontaise in Lausanne, and it was the host nation who got off to a winning start with a 2-1 victory, Italy's goal coming in the 44th minute thanks to Giampiero Boniperti. Two goals either side of it from Robert Ballaman and Josef Hügi put paid to any Italian winning start to the tournament. This would not be the last time that the two countries would meet in the group stages, though.

Italy's next game was played on 20 June against Belgium at the Cornaredo Stadium in Lugano, and it was a convincing win for them, 4-1. Léopold Anoul's goal for Belgium in the 82nd minute proved to be a mere consolation, as Italy ran rampant with four goals, with Egisto Pandolfini, Carlo Galli, Amleto Frignani and Benito Lorenzi inflicting the damage. On the same day, Switzerland lost to England 2-0. This meant that both Italy and the hosts had three points each and therefore a play-off match was arranged on 23 June in Basel at the St Jakob Stadium.

Josef Hügi and Robert Ballaman had been the main protagonists in the opening match for the host nation and would inflict further damage to knock Italy out of the World Cup at the group stage for the second consecutive time. Hügi scored a brace and Jacques Fatton got the other in a 4-1 victory, Fulvio Nesti providing the one bright spark for the Italians on an otherwise miserable evening for them.

West Germany would go on to win the competition for the first time, beating Hungary 3-2 on 4 July with four of the goals coming in the first 20 minutes.

Qualifying for the next World Cup in Sweden took place from January 1957 and ran for 12 months. Italy were paired with Northern Ireland and Portugal in UEFA Group 8. Unsurprisingly, Italy were under new management with the technical commission consisting of Angelo Schiavio, Luciano Marmo, Giuseppe Pasquale, Luigi Tentorio and Vincenzo Biancone, with the coaching managed by Alfredo Foni.

The committees for the 1950 and 1954 World Cup campaigns had failed to get Italy out of the group stages in the finals. This time, the present incumbents would not even reach the finals.

1958
Federal Technical Commission: Angelo Schiavo, Luciano Marmo, Giuseppe Pasquale, Luigi Tentorio, Vincenzo Biancone
Coach: Alfredo Foni

The qualification campaign got off to a winning start as Italy beat Northern Ireland 1-0 on 25 April 1957 in Rome, with Sergio Cervato converting after just three minutes. It was the return leg that would gain notoriety. Before that, there were two matches against Portugal and these games were firmly in the 'tit-for-tat' category. Firstly, Portugal won their home match 3-0 on 26 May, and Italy exacted revenge by the same scoreline on 22 December, with a brace from Guido Gratton and another from Gino Pivatelli settling matters. These two consecutive games against the Portuguese were not originally scheduled this way, as the return leg in Northern Ireland was due to be played on 4 December. The match did in fact take place, but not as a World Cup qualifier, and it famously became known as 'the Battle of Belfast'.

The first issue encountered before the match centred around the referee assigned to it. Dense fog had stopped Istvan Zolt getting from Hungary to Belfast. He had successfully flown from Hungary to London, but the connection to Belfast was suspended as the fog simply would not lift. An alternative official was sourced but by the time a firm decision was made, English referee Arthur Ellis could not make the necessary travel arrangements. The situation was now a desperate one as the Irish FA offered to send a local referee, but this was declined by their Italian counterparts, the result being that FIFA had no choice but to class the match as a friendly with the important qualifier to be rescheduled in the early part of 1958.

All of this had been done without notifying the people attending the match, with some finding out minutes before kick-off. Thousands of ship workers had been given time off to attend, causing consternation on the terraces – so much so that when the Italian anthem was played, it was not well received by the home crowd. This prompted the Italian team to react, with fierce tackles flying in and punches being thrown during the game. The situation threatened to get out of hand with the police having to stop the angry fans getting on the pitch. The match finished 2-2 and some of the Irish players helped their Italian counterparts to the relative safety of the dressing room. It was an escalation caused by frustration that was attributable to Mother Nature and a slow decision-making process, and it wasn't of the making of either the Italian players or the Irish fans.

The rescheduled match on 15 January was notable for a larger than normal police presence. Northern Ireland needed to win, while a draw would be good enough for Italy. The stakes could not have been higher as both countries took to the pitch in front of a crowd of 50,000 at Windsor Park, and it would be the home fans celebrating at the end of the match with Northern Ireland winning 2-1, with Jimmy McIlroy and Wilbur Cush putting the hosts two up within the half-hour. Dino da Costa halved the deficit with just over half an hour to go, but the Irish held on to secure a famous victory and progress to the finals at the expense of the Italians.

If the 1930s had been prodigious for Italian football, then the 1950s had witnessed the complete antithesis. It prompted the rest of the world to question Italy's standing: were they now a spent force? This wasn't the case in Italy though. The almost impossible replacement of Pozzo, the Superga tragedy, the processes followed by the technical committees and their ever-changing rank and file were salient factors in mitigation. They had all taken their toll and would require more time, and as the 1950s made way for the 1960s, Italian football at international level was not swinging.

1962
Federal Technical Commission: Paolo Mazza, Giovanni Ferrari

Since Europe had hosted the last two World Cups, and with the American federations saying they would boycott a third consecutive tournament in Europe, it was back to South America for the 1962 event, with the chosen destination being Chile.

Italy's route to the finals would see them paired with Romania, Israel, Cyprus and Ethiopia in Group 7, and each tie was played home and away. Rather strangely, the group was split into a first, second and final round with nations coming in at various stages. The only game in the first round saw Israel defeat Cyprus 7-2 over the two legs and their reward for doing so was a two-legged affair with Ethiopia. Italy were drawn against Romania but did not actually play the games due to the Romanians withdrawing from the competition, so Italy reached the final round without actually kicking a ball in anger. There, they would play Israel, who had seen off the Ethiopian challenge with a 4-2 aggregate victory, therefore being the only nation to actually participate in every round. The final round, first leg was played on 15 October 1961 in Tel Aviv. Israel's winning run to the final looked set to continue as they took a firm hold in the first half, to lead 2-0, the goals coming from Nahum Stelmach and Roby Young. However, a storming second half from the Azzurri saw them take control to win the first leg 4-2, Francisco Lojacono and José Altafini restoring parity before two late goals from Mario Corso settled matters. The second leg took place in Turin on 4 November with the Italians scoring six goals without reply to qualify for Chile, winning 10-2 on aggregate. It was a great match for Omar Sívori as he scored four of them with support from Corso and Antonio Valentín Angelillo. Both Sívori and Angelillo were Italian/Argentines, known as *Oriundo*.

Italy's first match in the finals was played at the Estadio Nacional in Santiago on 31 May 1962 in Group 2. Their opponents were West Germany. The match finished 0-0 and as befits many games with that scoreline, it was largely uneventful.

However, the next match at the same stadium just two days later was anything but, and not for the right reasons. Italy had played in previous matches that were filed under 'the Battle of …', but none of them had the impact or notoriety that occurred on 2 June, when 'the Battle of Santiago' took place against the host nation, Chile. Firstly, fuel was poured on to the fire by two Italian journalists called Antonio Ghirelli and Corrado Pizzinelli (writing for *La Nazione* and *Corriere della Sera).* They had written a series of articles that had angered the Chilean population. They claimed, 'the phones don't work, taxis are as rare as faithful husbands, a cable to Europe costs an arm and a leg and a letter takes five days to turn up', and said Chile's population was prone to 'malnutrition, illiteracy, alcoholism and poverty. Chile is a small, proud and poor country: it has agreed to organise this World Cup in the same way as Mussolini agreed to send our air force to bomb London [they didn't arrive]. The capital city has seven hundred hotel beds. Entire neighbourhoods are given over to open prostitution.

This country and its people are proudly miserable and backward.'

The Chilean press were quick to respond, describing Italians in general as fascists, Mafiosi, oversexed, and, because some of Inter Milan's players had recently been involved in a doping scandal, they were called drug addicts to boot!

A couple of days before the match was due to take place, an Argentine journalist had been severely beaten and hospitalised, having been mistaken for an Italian. Italian supporters were then barred from Chilean drinking establishments and even the Italian players were subjected to heckling from the local populace of Santiago.

Chile won the game 2-0, which effectively knocked Italy out at the group stages (this was confirmed the following day, after West Germany had beaten Switzerland 2-1 at the same stadium). The match was littered with the foulest of play almost from the first few seconds, with Italian midfielder Giorgio Ferrini being sent off for kicking an opponent in full view of the referee, but refusing to leave the field, citing that he had been continually kicked by the Chile players. He eventually had to be escorted off by the Chilean police.

The authorities' intervention was required a few more times as the match wore on. Italy's plight was made worse when Mario David received his marching orders after aiming a flying boot to the head of Chile's Leonel

Sánchez, also in full view of the referee. Just before this occurred, Sánchez had been lucky to escape a red card himself after delivering a left hook to the Italian defender's head. It was more in line with a boxing match as opposed to a football one and he was also lucky not to receive another red card after yet another left hook that broke the nose of Italy's Humberto Maschio. In truth though, both sets of players were guilty of some of the worst tackles and fouls ever witnessed in a game at the highest level.

The BBC in the UK showed the highlights of the match and the programme was introduced by David Coleman who proclaimed to the audience, 'The game you are about to see is the most stupid, appalling, disgusting and disgraceful exhibition of football in the history of the game. This is the first time these countries have met; we hope it will be the last.'

Coleman continued, 'The national motto of Chile reads, "By Reason or By Force". Today, the Chileans were not prepared to be reasonable, the Italians only used force, and the result was a disaster for the World Cup.'

Chile won the match with a looping header from Jaime Ramírez in the 73rd minute and a long-range shot from Jorge Toro with three minutes remaining.

There would be one more game for the Italians to play and pride was somewhat salvaged when they defeated Switzerland 3-0 to finish the group in third place with West Germany and Chile going through. None of these countries were triumphant ultimately though, as Brazil successfully defended their title (as

Italy had done in the 1930s) by beating Czechoslovakia 3-1 in the final.

Coleman was not to get his wish, as the 1966 finals once more saw Chile play Italy in the group stages. The eighth tournament was played in England, but first the Italians had to qualify for the finals and were placed in a group alongside Scotland, Poland and Finland.

1966
Manager: Edmondo Fabbri

Italy's first qualifying game was a 2-0 away win in Finland on 23 June 1965. Italy only conceded one goal on their travels during qualifying and that came against Scotland, who beat them 1-0. The other match saw a goalless draw played out in Poland. Home form was crucial for Italy. They amassed 17 goals, conceding just three during the campaign and optimism was high as the finals began on 11 July 1966.

Italy were drawn against the Soviet Union, Chile and North Korea in Group 4, and were strongly backed to progress from the group. The Azzurri got off to a perfect start with a 2-0 victory against Chile on 13 July at Roker Park, the home of Sunderland. Whilst the match was a physical encounter, it had nothing on their last battle in Santiago, four years previously. Revenge was gained with goals from Sandro Mazzola and Paolo Barison securing victory.

The next match saw the Italians face the Soviet Union, again at Roker Park. The only goal of the match came from Igor Chislenko to maintain the USSR's winning start to the tournament. This meant that Italy needed a victory against the East Asian country to go through to the knockout stages for the first time since 1938.

Italy's third and final game of the group stages took place at Ayresome Park, the home of Middlesbrough, on 19 July. The result was one of the biggest shocks in football history as a single goal from Pak Doo-ik just before half-time ensured a victory that saw North Korea qualify as runners-up to the Soviet Union, who maintained a 100 per cent record with a 2-1 win against Chile. North Korea had been dismissed and described as 'unglamorous, unfancied and unknown'. Italy had twice been World Champions and was arguably the worst result in 56 years of Italian international football. The golden years of the 1930s seemed more like centuries ago, as opposed to decades. The rot had set in during the start of the 1950s and 1966 would be the year that Italy reached their nadir.

The Soviet Union went on to reach the semi-finals before they were beaten by West Germany, who finished as runners-up in the final, beaten by England, who won the competition for the first time and on home soil, winning the match 4-2 after extra time.

The Italians weren't the only major team who had failed to reach the knockout stages and perhaps given that Brazil had won two consecutive World Cups, the shock of the South American failure rippled further than it had done in Italy. After all, Italy had not played knockout games in the World Cup for 28 years.

Both countries would make amends in the next World Cup, which was once more held in South America – this time in Mexico.

1970
Manager: Ferruccio Valcareggi

For this qualifying tournament, Italy were grouped with Wales and East Germany. Italy's first game was in Wales, and they got off to a winning start with a 1-0 victory courtesy of 'Gigi' Riva, considered to be one of the best players of his generation, as well as one of the greatest strikers of all time. The enigmatic centre-forward would continue his fine goalscoring run with two further goals in a 2-2 draw in East Germany. The final two games were home matches and Italy marched to Mexico in top spot with convincing victories to boot, firstly by beating Wales 4-1 in Rome and then defeating East Germany 3-0 a month later. Riva's sparkling form continued with three goals against the Welsh and one more against the eastern side of Germany to finish the qualifying campaign with seven goals in four matches.

If Italy had not found goals hard to come by in the qualifying group, then it was paradoxical in the group stage of the finals, with only one goal scored in the three matches that took place in June 1970 in Toluca and Puebla. Angelo Domenghini scored that goal in a 1-0 win against Sweden before two goalless games against Uruguay and Israel. Italy topped the group unbeaten and with four points with Uruguay also going through to the knockout stages in second place. It would be in these stages that Italy would once more excel in the opposing teams' territory.

Italy faced the hosts Mexico once more in Toluca on 14 June in the quarter-finals and won the match convincingly, 4-1. It was the Mexicans who took the lead though, when José Luis González Dávila opened the scoring on 13 minutes. Italy were back in the match 12 minutes later when Javier Guzmán put the ball into his own net. The second half saw the Italians take complete control with two goals from Riva and one from Gianni Rivera, whom the press had dubbed 'golden boy'. It certainly was a gold experience for his team and it was their first victory in the knockout stages of the World Cup since 1938.

It is not often that a plaque commemorating a match between two countries, played in a different one, proudly adorns the stadium it was played in, but that is the situation at the Estadio Azteca in Mexico City, where Italy faced West Germany in the semi-final on 17 June 1970 in front of a crowd of 102,444, and millions watching on TV all around the world. What unfolded in the 120 minutes of play passed into the highest echelons of football folklore and was also called 'the game of the century', *Partita del secolo*.

The match ended 1-1 in normal time. Italy had led as early as the eighth minute after Roberto Boninsegna had converted. In the 70th minute, West Germany's superstar defender, Franz Beckenbauer, dislocated his shoulder. However, he stayed on the pitch with his arm in a sling as the West Germans had already used their two permitted substitutions. It looked ominous for Italy's opponents, but with just seconds remaining, the unthinkable happened when another defender, Karl-Heinz Schnellinger, equalised. What made this even worse is that Schnellinger was plying his trade in Serie A with AC Milan. Soon after he scored, the final whistle was blown, signalling extra time would be played, and this is where the story really took off, with five goals scored, which still remains the record for the most goals scored in extra time in the World Cup.

A defensive mistake from Italy's Fabrizio Poletti in the 94th minute allowed Germany's goal machine, Gerd Muller, to give his nation the lead for the first time in the match. What made things worse for Poletti is that he had only recently come on as a substitute. Tarcisio Burgnich was to spare his team-mate's blushes just four minutes later when he equalised and then just a minute before the end of the first period, Italian hopes were raised once more with a brilliant effort converted by Gigi Riva (who else).

Back came Germany and Muller as his header made the score 3-3, but just one minute later, the match was finally settled in favour of the Azzurri, Gianni Rivera scoring after being left unmarked to meet a cross from Boninsegna. The move happened so soon after West Germany's equaliser that the TV coverage was still replaying Muller's second goal.

Italy were in their third World Cup Final, alongside Brazil, also celebrating a third appearance. Whatever the outcome, one of the countries would lay claim to be World Champions for a record third time. The stakes could not have been higher as both teams took to the pitch on 21 June 1970, once more at the Estadio Azteca in Mexico City with an attendance of 107,412.

The final really came to life in the 18th minute when Pelé headed Brazil into the lead, after a pinpoint cross from Rivellino. Roberto Boninsegna equalised for Italy in the 37th minute, after a mistake in the Brazilian defence. There were no further goals in the first half. However, the second half belonged to Brazil with their creativity and firepower overbearing an Italian side that was mired in a very cautious defensive system. A powerful shot from Gérson made it 2-1 on 66 minutes and the lead was stretched further just five minutes later. It was that man, Gérson, who assisted this time, with a long free kick that was headed down by Pelé into the flight path of the onrushing Jairzinho.

The game had witnessed some great moments, but the final goal that Brazil scored in the 86th minute will be forever the game's greatest memory. It was a true team goal that involved several key players, including Tostão, Brito, Clodoaldo, Jairzinho, Pelé and Gérson. The most significant passage of play centred around Clodoaldo, who beat four Italian players in his own half before passing to Rivellino on the left-hand side. Rivellino played an inch-perfect pass down the wing to Jairzinho who crossed the ball into the middle. The millions watching it on TV may have been forgiven for thinking that Pelé could have taken a shot himself, but to everyone's amazement, he held up play, allowing Carlos Alberto to overlap on the right-hand side and smash the ball home to make it 4-1.

It may have been a comprehensive loss in the final, but the Italians had reminded the football fraternity they were now relevant once more on the world stage. They had slayed the dragons that had either sent them out in group stages at the finals or had stopped them from reaching them at all. The question on everybody's lips was, could Italy actually bring back the trophy-laden years that they had experienced some 40 years ago, as the 1970s began in glorious technicolour?

1974

Manager: Ferruccio Valcareggi

The World Cup in 1974 was once more Europe-bound and this time it was the turn of West Germany to host the tournament. The qualifying group was kind to the Italians as they were paired with Turkey, Switzerland and Luxembourg, making the Azzurri the firmest of favourites to qualify for the finals. It came as no surprise that they qualified with ease, winning four games from six and drawing the other two. The most telling stat was that no goals were conceded, with 12 scored and seven of them attributable to Riva. The biggest winning margin came against Luxembourg in Genoa on 31 March 1973, Riva scoring four goals and Rivera bagging the other.

Italy's claim to be the doyens of defending continued in the friendly matches that led up to the finals. Most telling was a 1-0 victory against England at Wembley on 14 November, Fabio Cappello scoring the goal that made history as this was their second win (both friendlies) in a calendar year against the country that had given them modern football.

Italy had not conceded a goal since 20 September 1972 (a 3-1 win against Yugoslavia) as they took to the field to play their first match in the group stages of the finals on 15 June 1974 against Haiti at the Olympiastadion in Munich. Italy were not only favourites to win Group 4, but also to win the tournament itself.

No goals were scored in the first half, but it took just seconds of the second period for this to change. The opening goal sent shockwaves as it was the underdogs who prospered when the ball was played to Emmanuel Sanon, who kept his footing before rounding Dino Zoff to put Haiti into the lead. Italy were level just minutes later when Rivera's first-time shot hit the net after a scramble in the Haiti penalty area. Italy sensed blood and went into the lead for the first time with a shot from outside the box on the right-hand side from Romeo Benetti that took a deflection off the Haitian defence. Italy's labour was complete on 79 minutes when Pietro Anastasi scored with a right-foot toe-poke to make the score 3-1.

Italy's second match was against Argentina, which was played in Stuttgart and ended in a 1-1 draw with an

Argentine scoring both goals. René Houseman opened events in the 20th minute with Roberto Perfumo putting into his own net 15 minutes later. The final group match for Italy took place once more in Stuttgart, on 23 June. Their opponents were Poland with Argentina and Haiti kicking off at the same time. Every nation save Haiti could make the second-round group stage, but only two could go through. Argentina were clear favourites to win their match, so the Poland v Italy fixture was billed as winner takes all. The deadlock was broken in the 38th minute when a bullet header from Andrzej Szarmach found the back of the net to give the Poles the lead and this was further extended just before half-time with a beautiful strike from Kazimierz Deyna on the edge of the penalty area. The score remained 2-0 until five minutes from time when Fabio Cappello pulled a goal back. There were no further goals as Poland won the match 2-1 and therefore progressed to the second round at the expense of Italy, who had slipped back into the bad habits that had mocked them in the 1950s and 1960s. Poland reached the last four and went on to win the third-place play-off against Brazil, whilst West Germany were victorious in the final on home soil, winning 2-1 against Holland.

1978

Manager: Enzo Bearzot

Italy were once more paired in the same qualifying group as Luxembourg. Joining them were Finland and also England. England had not qualified for the 1974 tournament, and this added spice to the proceedings that were to follow in Group 2 from June 1976 to December 1977.

As expected, it became a two-horse race between the Italians and the English in order to finish first in the group and qualify for the 1978 World Cup, which was being held in Argentina. In the end it was decided on goal difference with both Italy and England finishing the campaign on ten points with one defeat and five victories. Italy's goal difference was plus-14 against England's plus-11. The games between them had been very close as well, with 2-0 home victories recorded in both matches. The first of them, contested on 17 November 1976 in Rome, featured goals either side of half-time scored by Giancarlo Antognoni and Roberto Bettega. Almost a year after the first match came the English victory at Wembley, with a header from Kevin Keegan in the first half followed by a goal from Trevor Brooking in the second period.

Destiny was firmly in the hands of the Italians who still had one game left to play, against Luxembourg. The final group game was played in Rome on 3 December 1977 and was over as a contest before it had really begun, with Italy scoring two goals in the first 11 minutes, Bettega and Francesco Graziani inflicting the damage. However, the expected goal rush did not materialise except for a third goal scored in the 56th minute by Franco Causio. The 3-0 victory meant Italy would be boarding the Argentina-bound plane in the summer of

1978 at the expense of England, who had now failed to qualify for two consecutive tournaments.

For the finals, Italy were drawn in Group 1 alongside the hosts, France and Hungary. The build-up to the finals had not been favourable for the Italians, with three friendly matches being played in which they had been largely unconvincing, with a defeat against Spain and draws with France and Yugoslavia. However, they put this right when it really mattered with three wins to top Group 1 and advance to the second phase. The first game pitted Italy against the French, and even though the Azzurri were favourites, France (playing in their first tournament since 1966) opened the scoring in the first minute when Didier Six was able to run down the wing before crossing the ball for Bernard Lacombe to place his header beyond Dino Zoff. This prompted Italy to start playing on the front foot as they began to dominate possession, and the rewards were to follow with a deserved equaliser midway through the first half. That goal was scored by Paolo Rossi and the winner came in the 54th minute with a shot from Renato Zaccarelli which found the net to give Italy a deserved victory in Mar del Plata.

The second match was also played at Estadio José María Minella, four days later, on 6 June 1978, against Yugoslavia. Italy made a nervy start, but two goals in a minute from Rossi and Bettega settled them down. A third was brilliantly claimed by Romeo Benetti on the hour mark. Italy were now in full control and hit the crossbar on several occasions. A penalty converted by András Tóth in the 81st minute meant that Italy won the match 3-1 and had qualified with a game to spare, as had Argentina. Those two nations took to the field in the final group game at the Estadio Monumental in Buenos Aires on 10 June. A Roberto Bettega strike from just inside the Argentinian penalty area in the 67th minute was enough to give victory to the Italians and to top the group.

The World Cup was now split into two groups of four nations. The winners of the group would go on to contest the final and the runners-up would be in the third-place play-off. Italy were drawn to play Austria, West Germany and Holland in an all-European affair. The first round of matches took place at the same time on 14 June. Holland completely dominated the Austrians, winning the match 5-1. In contrast, Italy and West Germany played out a 0-0 draw, putting Holland top of the group after matchday one. The second matches took place on 18 June, with West Germany once more proving to be the draw specialists with an entertaining 2-2 game against Holland. A Paolo Rossi goal scored after some beautiful link-up play and a mistake in the Austrian defence in the 13th minute, was enough to give Italy a 1-0 win.

This meant that the final group game between Italy and the Netherlands was now a de facto semi-final match, which was played in Buenos Aires on 21 June. An Italy win would seal a final berth, with the Dutch being able to afford a draw providing that the Germans did not win their match. Italy drew first blood in the 19th minute with an unfortunate own goal scored by Ernie Brandts as he tussled with Roberto Bettega. The lead lasted until the 49th minute when Brandts went from zero to hero with a fierce shot to bring Holland back into the game. The match was firmly in the balance with a winning goal from either team enabling an appearance in the final, and this opportunity came with 14 minutes to go. Holland, under the guidance of midfielder Arie Haan, were becoming cognate with long-range efforts during the tournament. Haan unleashed a shot from 30 yards which sailed past Zoff before going in off the left post to give his country a victory that once more saw them play the host nation in a World Cup Final.

Just like in 1974, it would be a home victory, with Argentina becoming champions for the first time, with a 3-1 win after extra time.

Despite defeat to the Dutch, Italy would be compensated by contesting the third-place play-off against Brazil (Austria had surprisingly beaten West Germany in their final match) on 24 June. Italy took the lead in the 38th minute, Franco Causio scoring the goal before two second-half goals from Nelinho and Dirceu turned the match in favour of the Brazilians, who won the play-off 2-1.

1978 had witnessed a much better effort from the Italians as opposed to four years previous. They had rediscovered winning ways once more with Paolo Rossi scoring three goals in the tournament. Both the individual and the nation had plenty to look forward to for the next World Cup which would take place in Spain, back on European soil.

1982
Manager: Enzo Bearzot

For the third consecutive World Cup qualifying, Italy were paired with Luxembourg and both nations would also face Denmark, Greece and Yugoslavia in Group 5. It was almost like the proverbial 'game of two halves' for the Italians as they won their first four matches all by the same scoreline of 2-0. A victory away at Luxembourg was followed up with home wins against Denmark and Yugoslavia before victory in Athens meant that they topped the group, scoring eight goals and conceding none.

All of these games had been played in 1980, but it was the qualifying matches in 1981 that caused consternation as Italy picked up just two points from the next three matches. A 3-1 defeat in Denmark was followed up with 1-1 draws against Yugoslavia and Greece. Italy were back to winning ways in the final game with a slender 1-0 victory at home to Luxembourg on 5 December. They had already qualified before the match took place but had been demoted into second place, finishing a point behind Yugoslavia, who topped the group on 13 points. Italy had scored 12 goals during the campaign and had conceded just five. It was a real team effort for the Italians, with the goals shared between them.

However, the star of Italy's 1978 World Cup had not been amongst them. Paolo Rossi had been given his Italian debut in December 1977 under Enzo Bearzot. His three goals in the finals in Argentina (playing in a three with Bettega and Causio) had brought him to the attention of the world, although he had made his name in Italy with 60 goals for Vicenza in just 94 appearances before and after the World Cup. A loan move to Perugia in the 1979/80 season brought him attention that was not desired by him or Italian football in general. Rossi was involved in the infamous 1980 betting scandal known in Italy as '*Totonero*'. The match-fixing allegations involved clubs in Serie A and B. The clubs were Avellino, Bologna, Lazio, Milan, Perugia, Palermo and Taranto, and all were declared guilty after the trials. The most notable footballer involved was Rossi. Initially the forward was banned for a three-year period, but that was later reduced to two years. Rossi always claimed he was innocent of all charges. His return to the game was with Juventus and he was able to play for the Turin giants at the end of the 1981/82 season, scoring one goal. This was enough for Enzo Bearzot to recall him into his squad for the upcoming World Cup finals.

The biggest change to the World Cup format in 1982 was that the finals now had 24 countries participating and for the first time all six confederations had nations representing them. Making their debut were Kuwait,

Algeria and New Zealand. Italy were placed in Group 1 alongside Poland, Cameroon and Peru.

Before a ball had been kicked, there had been concerns about the match-fitness of Rossi and these fears were compounded in the three games that Italy played at Balaídos, in Vigo. In fairness to Rossi though, the same could have been said about the team in general as they played out uninspiring draws in each game. Firstly, Italy played Poland with no goals scored on 14 June. This was followed up with a 1-1 draw against Peru. Bruno Conti opened the scoring on 18 minutes before Peru equalised through Rubén Toribio Díaz with just seven minutes remaining. Italy's third and final game in Vigo was played on 23 June. Italy once more took the lead, this time through Francesco Graziani before being pegged back a minute later when Cameroon's Grégoire M'Bida levelled matters.

In 1978, Italy had stormed their way into the second group stage. This time round, it had been more like a gentle breeze on a hot summer's day as they finished in second place, a point behind Poland. Italy's 'reward' was to be placed in a group with South America's superpowers, Brazil and Argentina, in the second group phase. Brazil had won all three of their games and Argentina (inspired by a young Diego Maradona) had won two. No one outside of Italy gave them a chance, and it is arguable that this was the case within Italian walls as well. The group was the definitive death one!

The first match came against the World Champions, Argentina, on 29 June at Sarrià Stadium in Barcelona.

The first half was notable for challenges that were committed rather than goalmouth action, but all this was to change in the 57th minute when the ball was played to Marco Tardelli, who found himself in a dangerous position in the Argentinian penalty area on the left-hand side. His first-time shot was perfectly placed to give the Italians the lead.

Argentina came close to equalising with long-range efforts from Daniel Passerella and a Diego Maradona free kick which rattled the post, and they were made to pay for this when Italy extended their lead in the 67th minute when Antonio Cabrini fired in after a great lay-off from Bruno Conti. Passarella made amends for his earlier miss with a free kick which sailed into the back of the Italy net to make it a nervy last seven minutes, but the Italians held firm (under the brilliant marshalling of Claudio Gentile, who had contained Maradona from start to finish) and their second phase group stage had got off to a winning start.

Argentina went out of the competition that they had won four years earlier, with a 3-1 loss to Brazil at the Sarrià Stadium on 2 July, before the final game of this fascinating group took place on 5 July in the same stadium, contested between Italy and Brazil. Both teams were on the same number of points, so a win either way would assure a semi-final berth. It promised to be a match that pitted Brazil's attacking *savoir faire* against intrepid Italian defending.

The match came alight as early as the fifth minute when Paolo Rossi opened his account in the finals, heading in Antonio Cabrini's cross. The game's second goal came just seven minutes later when Sócrates restored parity for Brazil, and it was now game on. Italy were back in front 13 minutes later when Rossi scored his second goal. The now rejuvenated striker intercepted a pass from Cerezo and drilled his shot into the back of the Brazilian net. There were no further goals in the first half, but the play was still relentless with Brazil attacking and Italy defending. The blue wall was finally torn down in the 68th minute of a pulsating match, when Falcão collected a pass from Júnior. Cerezo's clever dummy run at the same time took out three defenders and now Italy were exposed as Falcão seized the opportunity by firing home from 20 yards out.

This meant that Brazil were now in control of the group and would go through on goal difference if the score remained the same. The stakes could not have been higher as the match moved into its final act. The structure of the game had seen Brazil asking the questions and Italy answering them. In the 74th minute, Italy were awarded a corner which was poorly cleared by Brazil, the ball falling in the direction of both Paolo Rossi and Francesco Graziani, and both became predator-like, smelling blood and potential victory for their country. It was Rossi who got there first with his hat-trick well and truly assured.

Italy were 3-2 up and now in the ascendency again, and matters centred on the Brazilian riposte. This time though, it was a bridge too far and could have got worse for Brazil as Giancarlo Antognoni scored in the 86th minute, but the goal was erroneously disallowed for offside. Still the drama was not concluded, with Dino Zoff having the last word, making a wonderful save to deny Oscar a goal, and in doing so, sending Italy into the semi-finals, making up for what had happened in 1970.

The game was pure sensation, a work of art with a maximum of steel, and worthy of deconstruction several decades later.

Italy's semi-final opponents were Poland, and the match was played in Barcelona, but this time at the Camp Nou on 8 July. It was the second time that the countries had met each other as they had played in a very uninspiring 0-0 encounter on matchday one in Group 1 almost a month before. Zbigniew Boniek had been the main threat for the Poles leading up to the second clash, brilliantly supported by the likes of Grzegorz Lato and just like the Italians, Poland had grown into the tournament with momentum and belief. The difference between the two teams in the match was the player who had truly woken from his slumber in spectacular fashion against Brazil to reach this stage. Paolo Rossi scored in both halves to ensure Italy won the match 2-0, taking his tally to five goals in the tournament.

Italy were in their second final in 12 years and this time they would face the country that they had beaten in the semi-finals in 1970: West Germany. The Germans' route to the final had not been without its hurdles. They had topped their first group in the finals by beating Austria by a single goal to nil in the last game which meant that both countries would qualify. The game was largely played around the centre circle with both teams content not to play the ball into each other's danger areas, making the match far from entertaining. Germany's semi-final against France was the complete opposite, with both teams intent on going for it with the game finishing 3-3 after extra time, and West Germany winning the penalty shoot-out 5-4. However, the game was marred by a reckless tackle from West Germany's goalkeeper Harald Schumacher on France's Patrick Battiston. As a result, the Frenchman fell to the ground unconscious with a damaged vertebra and several teeth knocked out. The injury was so serious that Battiston slipped into a coma. Emergency medics had to administer oxygen on the pitch. Michel Platini later said that he thought that Battiston was dead, because 'he had no pulse and looked pale'. The referee did not even produce a yellow card for a tackle that many claimed was one of the worst of all time.

The final took place at the Santiago Bernabéu Stadium in Madrid on Sunday, 11 July. Chances were few and far between in the opening 45 minutes, with the defences coming out on top, although Italy really should have gone in at half-time with the lead when they were awarded a penalty that Antonio Cabrini meekly fired wide. The miss did not weigh heavily on Italian minds, and they took the lead in the 57th minute, Rossi scoring his sixth goal in the competition for his nation when he headed in from close range, assisted by Claudio Gentile's cross.

It was now up to West Germany to go on the offensive, but once again they were superbly marshalled by the Italian defence, allowing the Azzurri to exploit the situation with swift counter-strikes which soon saw Italy score two quick goals to take complete control of the final. Marco Tardelli's shot from the edge of the area beat Schumacher first to make it 2-0, before substitute Alessandro Altobelli made it 3-0. West Germany pulled a goal back with just seven minutes remaining through Paul Breitner, but this really was just a consolation for the 1974 winners. Soon afterwards, the final whistle was blown and Italy were crowned World Champions for the third time, equalling Brazil's record. Momentum had firmly been with the Italians since the second group phase and Dino Zoff became the oldest player to win the tournament as captain and at 40 years old.

Marco Tardelli's goal celebration in the final immediately found its place in football folklore, as he ran to the bench with fists clenched and mouth open wide, painting a landscape of pure fulfilled emotion. 'After I scored, my whole life passed before me – the same feeling they say you have when you are about to die; the joy of scoring in a World Cup Final was immense, something I dreamed about as a kid, and my celebration was a release after realising that dream,' he recalled. 'I was born with that scream inside me; that was just the moment it came out.'

1986

Manager: Enzo Bearzot

The 1986 World Cup finals were once more held in Mexico, as they had been in 1970. As champions, Italy did not have to qualify but did participate in the 1985 Ciudad de México Cup tournament, a prelude to the actual finals, also featuring the host nation and England. Italy won the cup by drawing with Mexico (1-1) and beating England 2-1 in their final game.

The preparation in friendlies leading to the finals was not textbook as they lost three games on the trot against Norway, Poland and West Germany before beating Austria and China.

The World Champions were placed in Group A and kicked off the tournament on 31 May with a 1-1 draw against Bulgaria. Alessandro Altobelli had scored the last goal for Italy in the previous finals in Spain and would be the first to do so in Mexico at the Estadio Azteca, just moments before half-time. The lead lasted until five minutes before the end of the match when Nasko Sirakov equalised for the Bulgarians. Once more, Italy's campaign had begun with a draw as it had done in 1982.

The second group match saw Italy take on Argentina at the Estadio Cuauhtémoc in Mexico City on 5 June, with the match once more ending 1-1. Altobelli gave Italy the lead from the penalty spot after just six minutes with Diego Maradona restoring parity (and gaining revenge somewhat for what had happened four years previously) with a goal just after the half-hour. The final group match took place at Estadio Cuauhtémoc on 10 June where Italy faced South Korea. Memories of a group defeat to North Korea in the 1966 finals were still fresh in Italian minds. This time though, Italy would come through, albeit in a very close match, winning 3-2, Altobelli scoring two more goals aided by an own goal from Cho Kwang-rae. South Korea made a game of it with goals by Choi Soon-ho and Huh Jung-moo.

Italy were then drawn against France in the round of 16 and this is where the defending champions' participation in the finals ended. France won the match 2-0 with goals in either half scored by Michel Platini and Yannick Stopyra in front of a crowd of 70,000 at the Estadio Olímpico Universitario on 17 June. The tournament winners were a Maradona-inspired Argentina, who beat West Germany 3-2 in a pulsating final, their second victory in just eight years.

1990
Manager: Azeglio Vicini

The last time that the finals had been played in Italy had been in 1934, so it was no surprise to see them once more host the tournament. During this finals, the 'beautiful game' became just that once more and this was no more evident than for England. The country had suffered severe hooligan issues on the terraces that spilled out on to the pitch during the 1980s. This didn't just happen on home soil but abroad as well, and one such incident ended in tragedy that went far beyond clashes between fans. The 1985 European Cup Final between Liverpool and Juventus took place at the Heysel Stadium in Brussels. Just an hour or so before the kick-off, it had become very apparent that aggression between the two sets of supporters was taking place close to an area of the ground which had been set up as a 'neutral' section. What initially began with object throwing soon turned to larger-scale physical encounters, forcing fans to flee. Mayhem ensued and ultimately led to a nearby wall collapsing with the deaths of 39 Italian fans recorded and a further 600 injured by the collapse and the crush that followed. Eventually the match was allowed to be played out with Juventus winning 1-0. The incidents sent shockwaves throughout the world of football. As a result, English clubs were banned from all European club competitions for five years – Liverpool receiving a further year on top of the generic ban. Italia 90 represented a new start for English football, and their team rose to the occasion.

As a result of hosting the tournament, Italy found themselves once more without a qualification role. Azeglio Vicini's preparations were fairly low-key with two friendly matches played in early 1990: firstly, a goalless draw in Holland, then a 1-0 victory in Switzerland.

Italy's campaign on home soil began on 9 June at the Stadio Olimpico with 73,303 fans in attendance, and the vast majority going home happy with a 1-0 victory, Salvatore 'Toto' Schillaci scoring the goal with 12 minutes remaining. This was followed up with another slender 1-0 victory over the United States five days later, but this time it was Giuseppe Giannini making his mark with a goal on 11 minutes. The group stage was completed on 19 June with a 2-0 victory (once more in Rome) against Czechoslovakia. 'Toto' Schillaci and a young and enigmatic rising star called Roberto Baggio made the difference with goals in each half. Italy had got off to a perfect start, with three wins, topping Group A comfortably, scoring four goals and conceding none in the process.

Italy's quest to become World Champions on home soil continued in the vein that they had approached the group stages – defend with stealth whilst ensuring devastation in attack. This is exactly what happened in the round of 16 against Uruguay in Rome on 25 June. Second-half goals from Schillaci (his third of the tournament) and Aldo Serena ensured safe passage to the quarter-finals. Their opponents were the Republic of Ireland, who had reached the stage by beating Romania on penalties. Thus far, Italy had registered wins either by 1-0 or 2-0, and it was to be the former once more with the zeitgeist's spirit wrapped around Toto Schillaci, his goal in the 38th minute separating the two countries as Italy progressed to the semi-finals.

The match was played in Naples on 3 July. Diego Maradona had played his club football for Napoli since 1984 and had transformed their fortunes, winning Serie A twice as well as the Coppa Italia and the UEFA Cup, and he had been the star player in the previous World Cup in Mexico. Naples was Maradona country and possibly the worst place for Italy to face his native Argentina to play for a place in the World Cup Final.

Italy had so far progressed by not conceding, with Toto Schillaci as the main target man who had scored the goals. The first half of the match very much followed this strategy with Italy leading 1-0 at half-time. A Gianluca Vialli shot was parried by the Argentine goalkeeper, Sergio Goycochea, into the path of Italy's leading scorer, who was quick to follow up.

However, a deft header from Claudio Caniggia in the 67th minute turned the game around. There were no further goals in regulation play or extra time and so the match was decided by penalties. Each country's first three penalties were converted before Roberto Donadoni's kick was well saved by Goycochea. Up stepped the mercurial Maradona, who duly netted to make it 4-3 to Argentina with one penalty each to go. The maths was simple – Italy had to convert their fifth penalty. Up stepped Aldo Serena but his effort was hit straight at the keeper. There was no requirement for Argentina to take their fifth as they were already through to contest the final at the expense of their hosts. The following night saw West Germany progress in an identical manner against England.

Italy won the third-place play-off against England with a 2-1 victory, but to the Italians this was a somewhat hollow victory compared to winning the tournament for the second time on home soil. West Germany won the final instead with a 1-0 victory against Argentina, which was a largely uninspiring spectacle to say the least.

1994
Manager: Arrigo Sacchi

The 1994 finals were held in North America for the first time. It would also be the first time that the final was decided on a penalty shoot-out – and the first time since 1982 that Italy had had to qualify to get to the tournament.

They were put into UEFA Group 1 which also included Switzerland, Portugal, Scotland, Malta and Estonia. The Azzurri topped the group with 16 points, with the Swiss also qualifying, with just one point less. Italy won seven of their ten games, with their only loss away to Switzerland on 1 May 1993 in Bern, Marc Hottiger scoring the game's only goal. Switzerland almost completed the double in Italy, racing into a 2-0 lead in the first 25 minutes in Cagliari, before two late goals from Roberto Baggio and Stefano Eranio earned Italy a draw, which had looked very unlikely for most of the match. It was a pivotal moment in the campaign.

The finals took place between 17 June and 17 July. Italy were one of the early tournament favourites with Roberto Baggio staking a claim for being the 'world's best footballer'. They were drawn in Group E alongside the Republic of Ireland, Mexico and Norway. It could not have been a tighter group, with each country winning, losing and drawing and with each finishing on four points and with zero goal difference. Mexico topped the group on goals scored – three – with Ireland and Italy finishing second and third respectively on two goals scored and separated by the result of their match. Norway's inability to score more than one goal was the reason that they were eliminated.

Italy's opening game had been against Ireland, with the Irish gaining revenge for the quarter-final defeat just four years previously. A Ray Houghton goal in the 11th minute proved decisive. This was followed up with a 1-0 victory over Norway, also in New Jersey, Dino Baggio netting in the 69th minute. The final game was against Mexico and finished 1-1, this time in Washington. Daniele Massaro opened his account three minutes after the break before Mexico forced their way back less than ten minutes later through Marcelino Bernal.

It had not been the most elegant of starts for Italy, but they had made it through the group stages and were now drawn against Nigeria in the round of 16 in Massachusetts on 5 July. It may not have been Independence Day, but the Italians were dependent on and grateful to Roberto Baggio who, in this game, showed why he was one of the greatest players at the tournament. Nigeria took the lead in the 25th minute through their winger Emmanuel Amunike with a close-range shot following a corner. It was a lead that lasted until the 88th minute, then Baggio received the ball just inside the Nigerian penalty area and coolly slotted it into the net with his right foot. The game went into extra time, and it was Baggio who won the match with his second goal, from the penalty spot, in the 102nd minute.

Italy were now up and running and faced a quarter-final showdown with Spain, once more in Massachusetts, four days later. Nigeria had taken the lead in the 25th minute in the previous game, and it was Italy's turn to go ahead at the same time with Dino Baggio hitting a stunning piledriver from 30 yards out. Spain were back in the game just before the hour mark with a smartly taken goal by José Luis Caminero from the edge of the penalty area. Roberto Baggio repeated his trick from the Nigeria game, scoring in the 88th minute to win the match for Italy and put them through to the semi-finals. Substitute Nicola Berti played the ball to Baggio who calmly ran into the penalty area before rounding the goalkeeper, Santiago Cañizares, to slot the ball home.

Italy were in the semi-finals for the fourth time in five World Cups. Their opponents were Bulgaria, who had been the surprise package in the competition. Hristo Stoichkov had been their talisman and had five goals to his name already. It was not going to be an easy game. The 25th minute had proved to be a milestone in the previous two rounds for Italy and by the time the clock showed that particular time, Italy were two goals to the good, both scored by Roberto Baggio, and both beautiful strikes. The goals brought him level with Stoichkov in the tournament. However, on the stroke of half-time, the Bulgarian scored his sixth goal, this time from the penalty spot, to provide his country with a lifeline for the remainder of the match. Despite there being a significant amount of the game to play, there were no further goals and once more, Italy found themselves in the final, where they would meet an old foe from the final in 1970.

Brazil had reached the final by finishing top of their group, beating Russia and Cameroon and drawing with Sweden. The knockout matches had seen them beat the USA, Holland and Sweden, this time winning 1-0 with Romário equalling Baggio's five goals in the tournament. The build-up to the final, which was played at the Rose Bowl in Pasadena on 17 July, centred around which of the hot-shots would come out on top. The truth was that at the end of the final, neither had. The final in 1970 between the two superpower nations of international football had been all about Italy searching for a way to win and Brazil showing the way, and it had been a spectacular showpiece that was worthy of the occasion. Now, 24 years later, the world witnessed the complete antithesis.

The pattern of the match was set as early as the fourth minute when Brazil's Mazinho fouled Nicola Berti and was booked. The first chance fell to Romario, whose header (from a cross by Dunga) was aimed straight at Walter Zenga, who did not have to do much to save it. Italy's opening chance soon came after some clever play from Daniele Massaro, who proceeded to beat two Brazilian defenders before finding himself one-on-one with Taffarel, but just like the header from Romario at the other end, he shot straight at the Brazil goalkeeper.

Both countries were forced into early substitutions with Brazil's Jorginho replaced by Cafu and Roberto Mussi replaced by Luigi Apolloni. The first half finished scoreless, as Gianluca Pagliuca denied both Romario and Branco.

The second half continued in the same way, with Brazil on top in terms of creating opportunities. Bebeto's header which was saved by Pagliuca was the best of what really were half-chances at most. The match was definitely being won in midfield with Dino Baggio for Italy and Dunga and Mauro Silva for Brazil, very much on top in terms of breaking up play. It was no surprise then that the match finished goalless. The pattern in regulation play continued in extra time, with Romario squandering a golden chance in the second period.

For the first time ever, the World Cup would be decided on penalties. Both countries missed their first spot kicks with Franco Baresi blazing over the bar and Pagliuca saving low to his right from Márcio Santos. The next four penalties were all converted to make it 2-2 with two penalties each to go – Demetrio Albertini and Alberico Evani netting for Italy and Romario and Branco doing the same for Brazil.

Italy's fourth kick was taken by Massaro and was saved by Taffarel to his left. Dunga was up next, and he duly scored to make it 3-2 to the Brazilians. The final Italian kick was entrusted to Roberto Baggio, who had been his nation's talisman throughout the tournament.

The maths was simple – score and it meant that Brazil would need to convert their fifth to win; miss and there would be no need for Brazil to take their fifth. Baresi had blazed over Italy's first penalty and Baggio did the same. Brazil had won the World Cup 3-2 on penalties and they dedicated their win to Ayrton Senna, the Brazilian triple Formula One motor racing champion who had lost his life at the San Marino Grand Prix less than three months before.

It may not have been a 4-1 thrashing like it had been in 1970, but the looks on Italian faces betrayed the presence of the same psychological cuts and bruises as 24 years earlier.

1998
Manager: Cesare Maldini

Cesare Maldini had been a prominent servant to AC Milan (primarily) and also played 14 times for the Italian national side. He was a defender who captained AC Milan when they became Serie A winners on four occasions, and also champions of Europe. His managerial career mirrored his playing one with a couple of spells as manager of AC Milan, amongst others. It was no surprise when he took the nation's reins for the World Cup in 1998, which was held in France (especially as he had done so well in charge of the under-21 team that had won a record three consecutive tournaments). In his side for the tournament was his son, Paolo Maldini – a family affair for the end of the century.

The last time that England and Italy had been paired in the qualifying group stages had been for the 1978 finals and now 20 years later they were once again drawn to do battle. It had been a very hard-fought campaign in the 1970s, with Italy claiming top spot on the same number of points but qualifying by scoring more goals than their English counterparts, and 20 years later there would be a similar tussle. However, this time the team in second place would be afforded the chance to still qualify through the play-offs, if they were one of the best-performing runners-up. Making up the rest of Group 2 were Poland, Georgia and Moldova.

This time it was England who topped the group after eight games, with 19 points, while Italy had 18. Both countries had started their campaigns with 100 per cent records, but it was Italy who turned the screw in the early months of 1997 with two important victories, firstly against England at Wembley on 12 February. The decisive moment came in the 19th minute when Gianfranco Zola beautifully controlled a long ball before unleashing a fine right-foot shot that flew into the net. There were no more goals and Italy's place at the top was further cemented with a 3-0 home victory against Moldova the following month. Italy were the only team with a 100 per cent record and looked very much like the nation that would qualify in first place. However, three consecutive 0-0 draws in the latter half of the qualifying campaign meant that Italy finished second in the group, and their chances of reaching the finals in France rested upon them winning their UEFA second round – this was where the eight best runners-up in the groups were placed into an open draw with matches then played on a home and away basis, with the winning nations over the two legs qualifying for the finals.

Italy were drawn against Russia, with the first leg played in Moscow on 29 October 1997. There were no goals in the first half but Italy drew first blood just after the break when Christian Vieri netted. The lead lasted for just a few minutes, then the unfortunate Fabio Cannavaro scored an own goal. The match finished 1-1 and there was all to play for in the return leg in Naples a few weeks later. The game was settled in favour of the home nation in the 53rd minute when Pierluigi Casiraghi converted to put Italy into the finals, 2-1 on aggregate.

The quest to go one step further than 1994 commenced on 17 June 1998 with an emphatic 3-0 victory against Cameroon in Group B in Montpellier. Italian nerves were eased as early as the seventh minute when Luigi Di Biagio netted and two second-half goals from the in-form Christian Vieri sealed the victory. Two further wins against Austria (2-1 with goals by Vieri and Roberto Baggio) and a 1-0 win against Norway (with Vieri making it four overall) sealed top spot, ensuring a quarter-final encounter with the hosts on 3 July in Saint-Denis.

Despite the location, Italy were classed as the 'home' team and took to the field in their familiar blue kit while France wore white. For 120 minutes the match was heavy on commitment but light on chances, with the midfield and defence of both nations coming out on top. The best chance fell to Roberto Baggio, whose chip over Fabien Barthez went just wide of the left-hand post. A place in the semi-finals was decided on penalties with the French going through 4-3. The final spot kick was taken by Luigi Di Biagio, whose fierce shot cannoned off the crossbar.

This was the third consecutive World Cup finals that Italy had gone out of on penalties, with the last two against the eventual winners. France won the competition for the first time on home soil, beating the 1994 victors, Brazil, in the final.

This match signalled the end of World Cup participation for Italy in the 20th century: a century in which they had totally embraced the competition upon entering it for the first time in 1934. They had participated in the finals on 14 occasions, winning it three times and finishing runners-up twice more.

The Italian impact on world football had been a significant one.

Now it was time to do the same as a new century dawned.

2002

Manager: Giovanni Trapattoni

Many Italian football correspondents and experts cite Giovanni Trapattoni as one of the most influential, successful and celebrated Italian managers of all time. It is not an arduous task to understand why this claim was made in the first place. Trapattoni was born in northern Italy in 1939 and served AC Milan with distinction as a central defender/defensive midfielder between 1959 and 1971. He also served the national side between 1960 and 1964. Trapattoni was part of the Italian squad that assembled for the 1962 World Cup finals but didn't actually play due to an injury he was carrying.

A fine student of the game, it was no surprise when he took to football management after retiring from playing in the early 1970s. He took the reins at his beloved AC Milan and moved on to Juventus (two spells), Inter Milan, Cagliari and Fiorentina, before becoming the national manager in 2000. It wasn't just in his native land that he made an impression either. Trapattoni also managed German giants Bayern Munich on two separate occasions.

Qualification for the World Cup finals, which were being held in Japan and South Korea, took place between September 2000 and October 2001. Italy were drawn against Romania, Georgia, Hungary and Lithuania in qualifying Group 8. The Italians were installed as the clear favourites to progress to the finals, and that is exactly what they did, with six wins and two draws, gaining 20 points in the campaign – four more than Romania, who finished in second place. The most noticeable thing was that Italy didn't concede a goal in any of the home games, winning all of them as well, with 12 of their 16 goals attributable to Filippo Inzaghi (seven) and the equally formidable Alessandro Del Piero (five).

One notable absentee from the pleasing qualification campaign was Roberto Baggio. The star of 1990 and 1994 had been carrying an injury. He declared himself fit for the finals themselves, but, Trapattoni did not see it that way and omitted him from the final 23-man squad. While this courted controversy, it could not take away the magnificent impact that Baggio had made on the national side in the 1990s, becoming one of the greatest players of all time.

Italy were placed in Group G in the finals and played matches against Mexico, Croatia and Ecuador. If the qualifying campaign had been one of consistency for Italy, then the finals were antipodal. A winning start against Ecuador in Japan was followed up with a defeat and draw in the next two matches. Two goals from Christian Vieri were enough to beat the Ecuadorians 2-0, but this was followed by a 2-1 defeat against Croatia. Once more, Vieri had given Italy the lead, with a close-range header from a great delivery from Cristiano Doni in the 55th minute. However, two goals in three minutes turned the game upside down. A tap-in from Croatian substitute Ivica Olić, after a mix-up in the Italian defence, levelled matters before Milan Rapaic looped a left-foot shot over Gianluigi Buffon. Italy were shell-shocked and Croatia were victorious.

Mexico and Croatia had the upper hand in the group and it looked ominous for the Italians when Jared Borgetti gave the Mexicans the lead after 34 minutes in their third and final group match on 13 June 2002. The other match, between Ecuador and Croatia, remained goalless in the first half and if nothing changed, Croatia would go through at the expense of the Italians. It was all to play for in the final 45 minutes. Soon after the break, Ecuador took a surprise lead, so many permutations were still up for grabs. However, Italy simply needed to at least get back in the match to salvage any chance of going through – especially in view of Croatia's win against them in the previous fixture. Croatia couldn't create another goal and found themselves on the losing side at the end of the game, and an 85th-minute equaliser from Del Piero changed the whole complexion with Italy going through in second place on four points, one more than Croatia. It had not been pretty, but Italy at least were able to progress.

Italy's reward was a second-round game against one of the hosts of the tournament, South Korea, in the round of 16. The match took place in Daejeon on 18 June in front of a crowd just shy of 39,000. As early as the fourth minute, the hosts were awarded a penalty which was squandered by Ahn Jung-hwan, who plied his trade in Italy with Perugia. This spurred Italy onwards and 14 minutes later they had taken the lead to silence the home supporters, Christian Vieri once more on the scoresheet. The lead lasted until the 88th minute when the South Koreans equalised through Seol Ki-hyeon, which sent the game into extra time and the home fans wild. Italy went down to ten men in the extra period when Francesco Totti was red-carded. Then, just as penalties were looming, a golden goal scored from the head of Ahn Jung-hwan sent the hosts through to the quarter-finals and Italy home.

The final was won by Brazil, who defeated Germany 2-0.

The result had shades of the defeat against North Korea in 1966. What made this even worse was that it was an Italian-based player who inflicted the damage, 36 years later. Italy, under the management of Trapattoni, had had the highest of hopes after such a convincing qualifying campaign. They had been firmly brought back down to earth in East Asia. Now it was time for a reset before the next World Cup back on European soil, four years later.

2006
Manager: Marcello Lippi

Paolo Maldini had made his full international bow in 1988 and during the next 14 years became a mainstay of the Italian defence. Son of previous Italian manager, Cesare Maldini, he played for his country 126 times and scored seven goals. Paolo took part in four World Cups, either playing at left-back or centre-half, and 2006 was the first onehe had missed since his debut. At 37, old Father Time had simply caught up with him. Although he never won the coveted trophy, Paolo had been chosen as one of the players of the tournament when Italy had come close to winning the competition for a fourth time. He had captained Italy for a record eight years and his 126 appearances was another record at the time. Paolo

Maldini would be overtaken in both of these lanes by two players that starred for the country in Germany in 2006.

Gianluigi Buffon and Fabio Cannavaro had both been part of Maldini's last World Cup adventure in 2002 – a tournament that had seen Paolo Maldini wear the coveted captain's armband. Now it was the turn of Cannavaro to do so.

Making his first ever World Cup finals appearance in 2006 was Inter Milan's midfield maestro, Andrea Pirlo. At 27, Pirlo was just coming into his prime. The nation hoped that he wouldn't be the only one.

There was a change in the hot seat as well. Italy had disappointed greatly in South Korea in 2002, despite having Trapattoni at the helm. Now it was the turn of Marcello Lippi to light the cigar for the Azzurri. Coming close to winning was no longer an option.

Lippi's playing days had seen him operate in a sweeper role and mainly for Sampdoria before hanging up his boots in 1982 – the year in which his beloved national team had last been crowned champions of the world. Lippi spent the rest of the 1980s learning the managerial trade and it was in the decade after that he really started to make his mark, with spells with Juventus (twice), Napoli and Inter Milan. It was no surprise when Italy turned to him in 2004.

Italy's path to Germany began in qualifying Group 5 alongside Norway, Scotland, Slovenia, Belarus and Moldova. Once more, Italy were clear favourites to qualify in pole position and this is exactly what they did, winning seven out of ten games and losing only once, to Slovenia away. Just like the previous qualifying campaign, it was at home where they really excelled, gaining a 100 per cent success rate. Italy finished on 23 points, which was five more than Norway. It was very much a team affair with no fewer than ten players contributing goals. Luca Toni was top scorer with four of them.

Group E in the finals welcomed Italy, Ghana, the Czech Republic and the United States of America. Italy got off to a winning start with a 2-0 victory against Ghana in Hanover on 12 June 2006, a goals from Pirlo and Vincenzo Iaquinta making the difference.

The next game was against the USA and was notable for the events that took place before the half-hour mark. Italy took the lead in the 22nd minute when a beautifully flighted free kick from Pirlo was met by the head of Alberto Gilardino. The United States were back in the match five minutes later when a free kick taken by Claudio Reyna on the right-hand side took a deflection off Cristian Zaccardo to make the score 1-1. Just one minute later, the Italians were down to ten men when Daniele De Rossi was sent off after elbowing Brian McBride in the face. This led to a four-match ban with McBride having stitches under his left eye. The match finished all square.

The Italians were back to winning ways with another 2-0 victory in their third and final group match, against the Czech Republic. Marco Materazzi opened the scoring in the 26th minute before the evergreen Filippo Inzaghi settled matters with just three minutes to go. It had been a solid start for the Italians, who topped the group with two wins and a draw to finish on seven points, a point above the surprise package, Ghana.

The round of 16 paired Italy with Australia and was played in Kaiserslautern. The match was settled in the very last few seconds of an absorbing tie when Italy were awarded a penalty after a foul on Fabio Grosso. Up stepped Francesco Totti to send his country into the last eight.

Their opponents in the quarter-finals were Ukraine and this time Italy didn't leave it until the dying seconds of the match, as they won 3-0. A brilliant long-range strike from Gianluca Zambrotta gave Italy the lead after just six minutes and it stayed 1-0 until just before the hour mark, when Luca Toni opened his account in the competition with a diving header to put the Italians in complete control. The same player was on the scoresheet ten minutes later when he tapped home after a tenacious run from Zambrotta. Italy won the match 3-0 and now faced the host nation, Germany, in the semi-final.

The Germans were under the management of Jürgen Klinsmann and were highly fancied to go through to the final on home turf after a 100 per cent record in the group and victories over Sweden and Argentina (on penalties) in the knockout stages. The match was played in Dortmund and was a very tight affair. Chances were few and far between with Buffon making important saves and Italy hitting the bar and post. It was no surprise when the game went into extra time, and it looked very much like it would be decided by penalties until Grosso curled a sweet left-foot shot into the net after Pirlo had played an inch-perfect short pass to him that seemed to deceive the German rearguard. There were still a couple of minutes remaining and Germany simply had to go for it and push everyone forward. One such attack was broken down, leaving Italy to score on the counter-attack and the match was settled by Alessandro Del Piero just before the final whistle was blown.

The final was contested between Italy and France at the Olympiastadion in Munich on 9 July 2006 with 69,000 fans in attendance. The game came alight in the first 20 minutes with both teams scoring. It was first blood to the French when they were awarded a penalty in the seventh minute when Marco Materazzi was judged to have fouled Florent Malouda. Zinedine Zidane was making his final appearance in an illustrious career that had seen the mercurial Frenchman play for Juventus from 1996 to 2001, and his 'Panenka' style kick went in after glancing off the underside of the bar. It did not take Materazzi long to make amends as his header levelled matters in the 19th minute direct from a corner from Andrea Pirlo.

It would not be the last time in the match that Zidane and Materazzi would make headlines.

Italy almost went ahead with a similar move to their first goal. This time, though, it was Luca Toni with a header from a Pirlo corner and unfortunately, the ball hit the crossbar instead of the net. The second half of the final was dominated by France, and they were almost awarded a second penalty, with Malouda once again challenged in the area, this time by Zambrotta, but the claim was waved away. Toni had been unlucky with his header that had hit the bar in the first half. His header in the 63rd minute hit the back of the net (Pirlo once again the creator with an inch-perfect free kick), but any celebrations were cut short when the goal was disallowed for offside. The match went into extra time and had now become a very tight affair with so much at stake.

Zidane came close to scoring the game's third goal in the 104th minute, but his header was tipped over by Buffon. Then, in the 109th minute the match was bathed in controversy that still reverberates today. Zidane and Materazzi were jogging up the pitch alongside each other. A brief exchange of words followed between the game's goalscorers before the Frenchman proceeded to head-butt the Italian in the chest and knock him to the ground. Originally, the incident had not been seen, and it was only when Buffon brought it to the attention of the assistant referee that action was taken. The game was held up as the referee (Elizondo) consulted with the fourth official via his headset. Zidane was sent off and the French were down to ten men.

The bizarre incident took the sting out of the game and as the final whistle blew, it was the second final in 12 years to be decided on penalties. Italy had fallen foul of this in 1994 and were determined not to make the same mistake this time around.

The only kick not converted came from France's David Trezeguet, whose thunderous spot kick hit the crossbar before bouncing back to safety. It was left to Fabio Grosso to convert the final kick to give his nation a 5-3 victory on penalties. It was fitting that he was the player to score the final and winning penalty, as he had won his side a last-second one in the round of 16 match against the Australians that gave Italy the momentum in the knockout stages.

Italy were World Champions for a fourth time and Lippi was now in the greatest of company alongside Pozzo and Bearzot. The old wave of Italian footballers like captain Fabio Cannavaro, Gianluigi Buffon and Alessandro Del Piero had blended superbly with the new wave, Andrea Pirlo, Francesco Totti and Luca Toni.

Italian football was presiding over matters at the summit of world football once more. Marco Civoli, a commentator for Italian TV channel, RAI, coined the following phrase, '*Il cielo è azzurro sopra Berlino*,' meaning 'the sky is blue above Berlin'.

The question now on everyone's lips was could the Italians create blue skies above other cities that would host the World Cups that were to follow in South Africa and beyond?

Or would they turn grey?

2010
Manager: Marcello Lippi

World Champions were no longer granted automatic qualification for the next finals and as such, Italy were drawn to play the Republic of Ireland, Bulgaria, Cyprus, Montenegro and Georgia in UEFA Group 8. For the third consecutive qualifying campaign, Italy came out on top. This time, the gap to second was extended to six points. Italy's record was seven wins and three draws, finishing the group with 24 points. Once more their home form was formidable, and they could even afford to drop points at home to the nation that finished in second place (Republic of Ireland) with the match finishing 1-1. Alberto Gilardino was top scorer with four goals, with eight other players making contributions as well.

For the first time in the history of the World Cup, the finals were held in South Africa and the bidding for the competition some years before had only been open to African nations. The finals were a complete disaster for the World Champions and made a mockery of how well the nation had performed to actually get there.

Italy were drawn to play in Group F alongside Paraguay, Slovakia and New Zealand. It would have taken a brave person to bet against the Italians comfortably progressing to the knockout phase, but this time fortune would have favoured them.

First up was a match against Paraguay in Cape Town. It finished all square with the Italians coming back from a

1-0 deficit in the first half to level matters via Daniele De Rossi in the 63rd minute. There were shades of qualifying from the group stages in 1982, with the results being all square, as in the second match, against New Zealand in Nelspruit, the score was 1-1, the same as the first match. Just like before, the Italians found themselves a goal behind before Vincenzo Iaquinta restored parity in the 29th minute from the penalty spot.

The final group game took place on 24 June 2010 at the famous Ellis Park stadium in Johannesburg. The permutations were extensive with all four nations in with a chance as Italy took to the field to do battle with Slovakia. As had been customary in the group, Italy found themselves a goal down and once more chasing the game, Róbert Vittek scoring in the 25th minute. It was the same player who extended his nation's lead with 15 minutes remaining and now the defending champions were desperately trying to climb a mountain to progress.

The deficit was reduced with just nine minutes left when Antonio Di Natale netted. Italy had hope and enough time to get back into the match as a frantic finish was assured. Indeed, there were two more goals scored but the decisive one came from Slovakia with just a minute to go. With Italy pushing forward, Kamil Kopúnek chipped Federico Marchetti with the Italian defence seemingly nowhere to be seen. The deficit was reduced once more with just seconds remaining when Fabio Quagliarella hit an exquisite shot on the edge of the penalty area to score, but soon the match was over, and

Italy were out of the World Cup, finishing bottom of the group with just two points. They only had themselves to blame. Their finishing in the final third was extremely poor, despite having a goal disallowed and a brilliant goalmouth clearance from the Slovakians.

In the final, Spain took the honours for the first time with a 1-0 victory in extra time against the most beautiful of football bridesmaids, Holland – the third time that they had been losing World Cup finalists.

2014
Manager: Cesare Prandelli

The appointment of Cesare Prandelli in 2010 was not met with the same enthusiasm as had been the case with Trapattoni and Lippi. Perhaps this was more to do with timing than anything else. The national team had gone from hero to zero in the space of four years.

He did not carry the same CV as his predecessors but there was no question that the former midfielder had changed the fortunes of Fiorentina between 2005 and 2010, where he had made them competitive in European competitions. He had steadied the ship so much for the club that his five-year tenure was the longest in the club's history and is still the case today.

The World Cup finals had moved from South Africa to South America with Brazil being awarded the 2014 finals. The samba beat was being played proud and loud.

The qualifying campaign began in UEFA Group B on 7 September 2012 with Italy playing Bulgaria in

Sofia. The match ended 2-2 with Dani Osvaldo netting both goals. Their last qualifying match took place on 15 October 2013. This time it was at home against Armenia in Naples. Italy's group campaign was bookended with another 2-2 draw, but six wins and two further draws in between had confirmed them as top of their group, with a six-point difference once more between them and second-placed Denmark. The other also-rans were Czech Republic and Malta.

For the finals themselves, Italy were placed into Group D alongside England, Costa Rica and Uruguay.

Italy had finished the 2010 finals in last place in their group, with just two points, but this was improved upon in their first match against England in Manaus, when they won the game 2-1. Claudio Marchisio had given the Italians the lead on 35 minutes. England were quick to regain their composure and found themselves back in the match just two minutes later via Daniel Sturridge, but Italy retook the lead through Mario Balotelli just after the break and the 2-1 advantage was maintained to the final whistle.

However, this was as good as it got for the Azzurri, as they suffered consecutive defeats to once more crash out of the finals in the group stages. A 1-0 defeat against Costa Rica was followed up with a defeat by the same scoreline against Uruguay.

Costa Rica and Uruguay went through to the knockout stages with Italy finishing third and England in last place.

Germany went on to face Argentina in the final, winning the match 1-0 just as they had in 1990. It was the third time those nations had met in the final.

The warm feeling of those blue skies that had embraced Italy in 2006 were now just a distant memory. The cold had crept in, and the skies were turning grey. Little did they know, as they began to look ahead to brighter days in World Cup competitions just over the horizon, that there would be severe weather warnings ahead of them that were much worse than they had ever encountered.

Italy and the European Championship: 1964–2016

PRIOR TO the introduction of the European Championship, there had been a number of tournaments involving several European nations. The first of these was the 'British Home Championship' which featured the nations that make up the United Kingdom: England, Scotland, Wales and Northern Ireland. Then there was the Central European International Cup which involved Italy, Austria, Czechoslovakia, Hungary, Switzerland, Poland and Romania. This competition ran from 1927 through to 1960. The final competition also involved Yugoslavia.

At the same time that the latter competition was coming to an end, a brand new one was about to make its bow.

The idea for a pan-European competition had been discussed in 1927 and was the brainchild of Henri Delaunay, the general secretary of the French Football Federation. However, it was not until 1960 that the competition came into being and Delaunay died a couple of years before its inauguration, but the trophy is named after him.

Rather fittingly, the first host nation was France. The first winners of the competition were Russia, who defeated Yugoslavia 2-1. There were 17 nations that had put their names forward for the qualification process. Italy was not one of them, alongside esteemed nations such as England, West Germany and Holland. By the time the second finals took place, in 1964, it was only the West Germans who continued to abstain.

1964

Manager: Edmondo Fabbri

Italy's first foray into the European Championship was a significant one as they were drawn to take on Turkey in a two-legged match to be played home and away in the qualifying stages. The first leg was held in Bologna on 2 December 1962. Fabbri had taken over the hot seat after the 1962 World Cup finals in Chile. His first competitive match was over in the first leg as his Italian side ran rampant, winning the game 6-0, Gianni Rivera scoring a brace, with the other four put away by Alberto Orlando, three of them scored in a blistering first half. The second leg in Turkey was a mere formality, with the Italians adding another goal to win 7-0 on aggregate, Angelo Sormani netting with just moments to go.

It was the same format in the round of 16. This time their opponents were the Soviet Union who were the reigning champions, and this told over the two legs with them winning 3-1 overall. A 2-0 defeat in Russia was followed with a 1-1 draw in Rome.

It had not been the start in the competition that Italy wanted. A finals berth would have been so much better. They would not have to wait much longer to reach the finals and go a step further by actually winning it, and all on home soil, just like in 1934 in the World Cup.

1968
Manager: Ferruccio Valcareggi

Valcareggi had originally served under the previous incumbent (Fabbri) and he took the reins alongside Helenio Herrera in 1966. A year later and the hot seat was his solely. This proved to be a wise choice as Valcareggi set about making Italy great again after years in the wilderness.

As befits new competitions, there were changes made to the qualifying rounds. Out went the preliminary round and round of 16, and in their place was a more recognised group format with matches still being played on a home and away basis.

Italy were drawn in the same group (6) as Romania, Switzerland and Cyprus. Their route to the quarter-final stage (the last before the actual finals) was an emphatic one with five wins and one draw, winning the group at a canter. The only team that they dropped points against were Switzerland as the match in Lugano finished 2-2 with Riva scoring both. He finished the group stages as top goalscorer with six in total.

The quarter-finals paired Italy with Bulgaria, who had topped Group 2. It was the Bulgarians who took advantage of playing at home in Sofia in the first leg with a slender 3-2 victory. However, this was overturned in the second game with Italy winning 2-0 in Naples on 20 April 1968. Pierino Prati (who had scored the decisive second goal in the first leg) restored parity with a goal on 14 minutes which was then followed up with the winner in the 55th minute courtesy of Angelo Domenghini.

Italy reached the finals with a 4-3 victory. Joining them for the four-team knockout tournament in Italy were England, the Soviet Union and Yugoslavia.

Italy were drawn to play the Soviet Union in their semi-final. The Russians had already built up history in the competition by reaching both previous finals, winning the first in 1960 and losing to the Spanish in 1964 (and they were also the nation that had knocked out the Italians in the qualifiers). Revenge was on the minds of Italy as both nations took to the field on 5 June 1968 in Naples. Before the meeting, Valcareggi had claimed that the Soviets, whilst having current superiority, were not unbeatable. Despite it being summer, the weather was atrocious and made for a physical encounter. The match ended goalless after 120 minutes of play. It was the game in which Dino Zoff came to the fore and cemented his place as Italy's number one goalkeeper for many years to come, as he made crucial saves, thwarting several players at crucial times. For the first and only time, the game was decided by the toss of a coin.

Italy's captain was Giacinto Facchetti, and it was down to him to win the call. The toss was made in the dressing rooms, witnessed by two administrators. Facchetti called tails and it was the correct choice. The 70,000 fans packed into the stadium waited with bated breath and were informed that Italy were through to the final when a jubilant Facchetti raised his arms to celebrate.

Italy's opponents in the final, played three days later in Rome, were Yugoslavia, who had beaten England 1-0. It was Yugoslavia who drew first blood in the 39th minute through their talisman, Dragan Džajić. The lead lasted until ten minutes before the end of the match when Italy were awarded a free kick just outside the penalty area. It was taken by Angelo Domenghini, who rifled the ball into the back of the net. The match was now finely poised at 1-1 and this was the final score after extra time. This time though there would be no decision made by the flick of a coin and the game went to a replay, once more held in Rome at the Stadio Olimpico. Just like with the coin toss, this was the first and only time this method of determining the winner occurred. To freshen things up, coach Valcareggi made five changes to the line-up.

Italy took the lead in the 12th minute through Gigi Riva when he was first to react in the penalty area after a miscued shot from Domenghini. The lead was increased in the 30th minute with what still remains one of the greatest goals in the competition. Expert Italian passing found the incomparable Pietro Anastasi just outside the penalty area. Anastasi flicked the ball up and volleyed it into the back of the net. Italy were now 2-0 up and heading towards their first European Championship success, which was confirmed just over an hour later. They became the first nation to claim both this trophy and the World Cup.

1972
Manager: Ferruccio Valcareggi

Under Valcareggi, the Italians had blown away the cobwebs of underachievement that had become customary in the 1950s and through to the latter part of the 1960s. They were European Champions and had reached the final of the World Cup in 1970.

Italy's group to qualify for the finals which were being held in West Germany in 1972 consisted of Austria, Sweden and the Republic of Ireland. Once more, the Italians were favourites to reach the quarter-finals. The smart money once again came up trumps as four wins and two draws meant finishing the group on ten points, three above their nearest rivals, Austria, and 12 goals were scored with only four conceded. The biggest wins enjoyed by the Azzurri came on home soil against the Republic of Ireland and Sweden, both matches ending 3-0. Five players contributed to the goalscoring charts: Roberto Boninsegna, Giancarlo De Sisti, Pierino Prati (all with three), Gigi Riva (two) and Sandro Mazzola.

Italy were then paired with Belgium for the quarter-finals, with home advantage in the first leg. The match finished goalless, so it was all to play for when both nations met in Brussels on 13 May 1972. Wilfried Van Moer gave the hosts a first-half lead with a powerful header in the 23rd minute. The lead was doubled in the 71st minute via a smart volley from Paul Van Himst. A penalty impeccably converted by Riva with just minutes remaining raised hopes of a second successive finals appearance and the chance to successfully defend the cup, but this was not to be, with the final whistle blown soon after. Italy had won the competition on home soil in 1968 and the same was just about to happen to West Germany, as they won the finals by comprehensively beating the Soviet Union, 3-0.

1976
Managers: Fulvio Bernardini & Enzo Bearzot
Ferruccio Valcareggi had made the Italian national side into competitors once more and had served his country well from 1966 to 1974. His tactics were rigid at times but very effective. They were inspired by the *catenaccio* system, and this had been made popular by the Inter Milan manager Helenio Herrera during the 1960s. This tactic made use of a sweeper behind the two central defenders and the full-backs. This gave rise to solid defending and stability. For the purists, this may have provided resilience but it was sometimes not aesthetically pleasing. This was of no concern to Valcareggi, especially during the 1970 World Cup in Mexico, where the altitude was an issue. The Italians were able to bring the ball out slowly and defend leads where they presented themselves.

It was not just in defence, however, that Valcareggi made his executive decisions. He also concentrated on matters where the more skilful players would come into play, and it was not uncommon for him to carefully employ the talents of Mazzola and Rivera at different times during matches. Mazzola was known for being the quicker and more dynamic of the playmakers and would start matches, while Rivera's talents would come into play further down the line of a match as he was able to dictate the play when the opposition tired. This was known as the *staffetta* tactic and served the manager well – but not so much in the 1974 World Cup finals, when his team played more direct and attacking football. Despite this, Italy were nowhere near as successful as they had been in Mexico. It was time for a changing of the guard – again.

Initially the role was given to Fulvio Bernardini but he was replaced by Enzo Bearzot as Italy's bid to qualify for the finals in Yugoslavia got off to a bad start with a 3-1 defeat in Holland and a goalless draw at home against Poland in Group 5 of the qualifiers.

It would be against the final team in their group that they would pick up their first victory with a slender 1-0 away win against Finland. A disastrous goalless draw at home to the Finns was followed up with the same scoreline away in Poland and even though the Italians finished the campaign with a 1-0 victory at home against the Dutch (who won the group on goal difference over Poland), the damage had already been done, rendering that final game meaningless for the Italians.

The finals were contested between Czechoslovakia, Holland, West Germany and the hosts, Yugoslavia. They were won by Czechoslovakia in Belgrade on penalties after a 2-2 draw in 120 minutes of play.

1980
Manager: Enzo Bearzot

The finals were held once more in Italy and they were the first to feature eight teams. The host nation didn't have to go through the qualifying process, which saw the top teams in the seven groups of four nations automatically qualify without having to play a quarter-final as had been the norm previously. It was also the last time that a third/fourth-place match was played.

The other nations joining the Italians were Greece, England, Holland, Czechoslovakia, Spain, Belgium and West Germany. The matches took place in Rome, Milan, Naples and Turin and the competition ran between 11 and 22 June 1980.

The Azzurri were drawn to play against Belgium, England and Spain in Group 2. Goalless draws had proven to be Italy's downfall in attempting to qualify for the 1976 European Championship, and that once more proved to be the case in the actual finals of 1980.

A 1-0 victory against England (Marco Tardelli scoring) was sandwiched in between 0-0 games against Spain and Belgium. Italy finished the group in second place behind Belgium, who had the same number of points, wins, draws and goal difference (plus 1) as Italy, but went through to the final to play West Germany as they had scored more goals. Italy would have to be content with a place in the third-place play-off match against defending champions, Czechoslovakia, in Naples on 21 June. There were no first-half goals and Ladislav Jurkemik gave the champions the lead on 54 minutes before Italy equalised in the 73rd minute through Francesco Graziani. There were no further goals in regulation or extra time, so the game was decided on penalties. The first 17 penalties were superbly executed by both nations, until Fulvio Collovati failed to convert, so the hosts lost 9-8 to finish in fourth place West Germany took the honours in the final with a 2-1 victory over Belgium in Rome, the day after Italy had finished in fourth place on home soil.

1984
Manager: Enzo Bearzot

Just like they had done in 1976, Italy failed to qualify for the finals that were held in France, despite being crowned World Champions two years before. Italy were placed into Group 5 alongside Romania, Sweden, Czechoslovakia and Cyprus. More nations had now been added to the qualifying roster.

It was a woeful qualifying campaign for the Azzurri with just one victory, which came in the final group match against the whipping boys of the group, Cyprus, on 22 December 1983. Before that they had recorded three draws and four defeats. Italy finished in fourth place, five points below Czechoslovakia, six behind Sweden, and seven behind table-toppers Romania. What made this even worse was that it was still only two points for a win and their 1-1 away draw against Cyprus came courtesy of an own goal scored by Nikos Patikkis after his nation had taken the lead. It was Italy's only point (and goal) scored on their travels.

Alessandro Altobelli was the leading scorer with two goals and the others were shared between Antonio Cabrini, Francesco Graziani and the star man of the 1982 World Cup, Paolo Rossi.

The championship was won by France for the first time on home soil with a 2-0 victory over Spain at the Parc des Princes in Paris on 27 June 1984.

1988

Manager: Azeglio Vicini

Only two of Vicini's squad for the championship were over the age of 30 and they were reserve goalkeeper Stefano Tacconi and, more tellingingly, Alessandro Altobelli, who was also the captain of the team. At 32, Altobelli was the only player with more than 50 caps. Making his bow in a major competition was Paolo Maldini, who was the youngest member of the squad at 19.

If goals had been a rare commodity in the previous qualifying campaign, then it was the complete opposite for the road to West Germany in 1988, as Italy scored ten more goals and finished as Group B winners to qualify for the finals. The other teams vying for a place were Sweden, Portugal, Switzerland and Malta. Italy recorded six wins and drew and lost one as they finished three points above Sweden.

The Azzurri wasted no time in righting the wrongs of 1984 as they scored their first goal of the qualifying campaign in the first minute of their opening group match against the Swiss in Milan on 15 November 1986, with Roberto Donadoni netting. The Swiss were back on level terms just after the half-hour mark through Jean-Paul Brigger, but two second-half goals from Altobelli settled matters despite Switzerland scoring late on via Martin Weber to make the final score 3-2 to the hosts.

This was followed up with two games against Malta. The first took place in Ta' Qali in northern Malta with Italy winning the game 2-0, Riccardo Ferri and Altobelli both scoring in the first 20 minutes. If Italy could be accused of taking their foot off the gas for the remainder of the match, then this was most certainly not the case in the return fixture in Bergamo. Italy won that game 5-0 with all the goals coming in a frantic first half that saw Altobelli continue his fine form with a further two goals (five in all so far) with contributions from Salvatore Bagni, Giuseppe Bergomi and Gianluca Vialli. Italy's claim for top spot was further strengthened with a 1-0 away win in Portugal to make it four wins out of four in the campaign. Once more it was Altobelli (who else) making the difference.

The one and only defeat in the campaign came in match five with a 1-0 win for Sweden in Solna on 3 June 1987, which was followed up with a goalless draw away in Switzerland a few months later. Any misconceptions of an Italian downturn were blown away with two home victories against Sweden (2-1) and Portugal (3-0) to finish top of the group with 13 points. It was no surprise to see Altobelli top the scoring charts with six, although there were no further goals from him in the remaining matches. Gianluca Vialli claimed four with Luigi De Agostini and Giuseppe Giannini added one goal apiece to those contributed by Bergomi, Bagni, Donadoni and Ferri.

For the finals themselves, Italy were drawn in a group with the hosts West Germany, plus Denmark and Spain. The opening game of the tournament occurred on 10 June 1988 in Düsseldorf when West Germany played Italy. The first goal was scored by Roberto Mancini in the 52nd minute before the Germans equalised just three minutes later via Andreas Brehme and the match finished all square, 1-1.

The Italians' next match came four days later when they took on the 1984 runners-up, Spain. The French had not qualified despite being champions. A goal from Gianluca Vialli in the 73rd minute settled matters. The third and final group game saw Italy beat Denmark in Cologne, 2-0, Altobelli and De Agostini making the impact.

Italy finished the group in second place behind West Germany, who qualified top by virtue of §having a better goal difference.

The semi-final draw pitched West Germany against Holland and the Italians versus the Soviet Union. The smart money was on a West Germany–Italy final, but it was the Dutch and the Russians who progressed instead, with Holland winning their game 2-1 and Russia winning 2-0 in Stuttgart, second-half goals from Hennadiy Lytovchenko and Oleh Protasov damaging the Azzurri.

Holland claimed the famous trophy with a 2-0 win in the final with goals from Ruud Gullit and Marco van Basten. The second goal from Van Basten is often cited as one of the greatest goals of all time, and not just in the final of the Euros, but in football in general.

Despite going out in the semi-finals, Italy's heads could be held high. They had scored plenty of goals in qualifying and the finals themselves and played some attractive football – and both scorers in the final were playing for AC Milan at the time as well.

1992
Manager: Arrigo Sacchi

A political wind of change had started sweeping through Europe in the latter part of the 1980s and early part of the 1990s. There was the reunification of Germany after the Berlin Wall was dismantled and that was part of a series of events that started the fall of communism in central and eastern Europe. This paved the way for the end of the Soviet Union as a superpower and with it, the independence of 15 states that were once part of it. The collapse of one-party state regimes made way for democratically elected governments in Poland, Hungary and Romania amongst others. The events in Germany were known as the 'Peaceful Revolution'.

In parallel, events in Yugoslavia provided the complete antithesis to those good feelings being expressed in other parts of the continent. The wars in the country were a series of separate (but related) ethnic conflicts, wars of independence and insurgencies. This resulted in the break-up of Yugoslavia in 1991 and the emergence of separate states that became known as Croatia, Slovenia, Bosnia and Herzegovina, Montenegro, Serbia and Macedonia (later to become North Macedonia).

Inevitably, all these movements would impact sport and the 1992 Euros held in Sweden was one of the first events to experience the very significant changes.

Italy would not be part of the finals though. One of five countries in qualifying Group 3, the Azzurri finished in second place to the Soviet Union with Norway, Hungary and Cyprus taking up the other positions.

Italy lost just one match in the campaign, against Norway in Oslo, 2-1. Their inability to turn draws into wins seriously impacted progression, as they drew four matches and won the other three. The three victories included the double against the group's whipping boys, Cyprus (who lost all eight of their matches), and a 3-1 home win against Hungary.

Italy finished the tournament on ten points and scored 12 goals, conceding only five. Roberto Baggio, Roberto Donadoni, Aldo Serena and Gianluca Vialli all scored two apiece with Attilio Lombardo, Ruggiero

Rizzitelli, Toto Schillaci and Pietro Vierchowod bagging one goal each.

The Soviet Union won the qualifying group but were known as CIS for the finals (Commonwealth of Independent States). There would be no more West (or East) Germany. Now simply known as Germany, it was this country that finished as runners-up in the finals. The winners were Denmark, who defeated them 2-0.

What made this victory even more remarkable was that the Danes had not originally qualified for the finals. Like Italy, Denmark finished in second place in their qualifying group. Yugoslavia had won Group 4 by a single point but were banned from playing in the finals due to the troubles taking place, which prompted the United Nations Security Council to impose sanctions on them. As a result, FIFA and UEFA suspended Yugoslavia on 31 May 1992, just weeks before the finals were played, and Denmark took their place.

1996
Manager: Arrigo Sacchi
England had hosted the World Cup in 1966, and 30 years later now hosted the Euros for the first time. There were also major changes made for the finals, with 16 nations participating, doubling the previous tallies. The break-up of the Soviet Union and Yugoslavia had an impact on the decision to allow more countries to participate.

Italy were drawn in Group 4 of the qualification process alongside a number of these newer nations:

Croatia, Lithuania, Ukraine, Slovenia and Estonia. The campaign was a very competitive one which saw Italy winning seven, drawing two and losing just one match. This record was identical to Croatia's, with both teams finishing on 23 points (another change was that nations were now awarded three points for a victory). Croatia finished top by having a goal difference of three more than the Azzurri.

Italy's only defeat came against Croatia on 16 November 1994 in Palermo, the irreplaceable Davor Šuker scoring a goal in each half before a last-minute Dino Baggio goal reduced the deficit. This was the only time that Italy had dropped any points on home soil, and apart from a slender 1-0 victory against Slovenia, the winning margins were considerable. Estonia were beaten 4-1 and Ukraine lost 3-1 in the penultimate qualifying match before Italy's comprehensive 4-0 victory against Lithuania in the final game. All four goals in the last match were scored in the second half, firstly via Alessandro Del Piero before a hat-trick from Gianfranco Zola completed the rout. Zola was Italy's top scorer with seven goals. Despite not coming top of the group, Italy's campaign was a robust one and they qualified for the finals as the best-placed runners-up.

Italy's finals group consisted of three other nations that only a few years ago would have been named differently. Germany would have been West and East Germany; Russia would have been the Soviet Union and the Czech Republic would have been known as

Czechoslovakia. Regardless of the political situations that came before, this was a very hard and competitive group to navigate.

Italy got off to a winning start at Anfield (home of Liverpool FC) on 11 June 1996 with a 2-1 victory over Russia. Pierluigi Casiraghi scored both goals, firstly, hitting a shot just outside the penalty area and then turning neatly into the box in the second half to fire the winner. Three days later and Italy were beaten by the same scoreline and in the same stadium by the Czech Republic, with Pavel Nedved scoring the first goal for the victors in the fifth minute. Italy were back on level terms through Enrico Chiesa before Radek Bejbl restored the lead for his nation, which they held on to. All three goals were scored in the first half. Italy's final group match came against Germany at Old Trafford (home of Manchester United). Germany had already qualified with two straight victories which meant that a win for Italy would be enough to see further progression, providing that they bettered the Czech Republic, who were facing Russia at the same time.

The match was played at a frantic pace with strong tackles made by both teams. Italy had a great chance to score when they were awarded a first-half penalty which was taken by Gianfranco Zola. It was not the best of strikes and was easily saved by Andreas Köpke. Italy's inability to take the chances that came to them during the match was to cost them dearly, especially with the second-half sending-off of German midfielder Thomas

Strunz, which should have provided them with even more opportunities. Germany held on, and it was the Czech Republic who also progressed despite drawing (3-3) against Russia. The 2-1 win afforded to the Czechs against Italy proved to be the decisive blow, despite Italy having a better goal difference.

The final was contested by the same two teams that had qualified from Group C, with Germany once again winning the tournament (and gaining revenge for the 1976 final) by beating the Czech Republic 2-1 with a golden goal in extra time scored by Oliver Bierhoff. It was their third win in the competition since its inception, their first as a unified Germany and their fifth appearance in the final.

Italy had only reached one previous final and that had been some 28 years since.

Now it was time to address the balance as the next tournament would take them into a brand-new century. A century when they would appear in three actual finals in just over 20 years.

2000
Manager: Dino Zoff

28 February 1942 will always be a significant date in the history of Italian football because it was the day that Dino Zoff was born.

During his playing career, Zoff set many records that were simply outstanding. The shot-stopper lifted the World Cup in 1982 and thus became the oldest player to do so, at the age of 40. He was voted the best goalkeeper and not surprisingly made the team of the tournament as well, an accolade that was afforded to him in the 1968 Euro finals too. He is the only Italian to have won both the World Cup and European Championship. Zoff's credentials in club competitions were equally outstanding: winning six Serie A titles with Juventus as well as two domestic cups and a European one (UEFA Cup), in 1977. Zoff also expertly represented Udinese, Mantova and Napoli.

His journey from player to manager was also impressive and he repeated the feat of winning domestic and European trophies (the UEFA Cup once more) with Juventus in the same season during the 1989/90 campaign.

Zoff was appointed as Italy's manager in 1998 and adopted a more attacking style of play and also started to introduce the younger generation on to the international stage.

The first finals of the 21st century were co-hosted by Belgium and Holland and for the qualifying campaign, Italy were placed into Group 1 alongside Denmark, Switzerland, Wales and Belarus.

It was a successful campaign with Italy finishing top of the group with 15 points – one more than Denmark. The Azzurri won four out of eight matches with three draws and only one defeat. Three out of the four victories came at the start of the campaign: a 2-0 win in Wales was followed up with a similar victory against the Swiss on home soil. A significant 2-1 victory in Denmark in their next match ensured a 100 per cent winning start with the Italians sitting pretty at the top of the table. The most convincing win came in match five with a 4-0 thrashing of Wales in Bologna on 5 June 1999. Christian Vieri started the rout with Filippo Inzaghi, Paolo Maldini and Enrico Chiesa also contributing.

Their only defeat took place a couple of months later against Denmark in Naples. It looked very much like an Italian victory when they went two goals up just after the half-hour mark through Diego Fuser and Vieri. However, the Danes were back in the game just before the 40th minute when they were awarded a penalty which was converted by Martin Jørgensen. Two second-half goals from Morten Wieghorst and Jon Dahl Tomasson ensured a 3-2 away victory and meant that Italy would need a point in their final match away in Belarus to qualify. This was confirmed with a 0-0 draw. Filippo Inzaghi and Vieri finished as joint top scorers with two each.

For the finals themselves, Italy were placed into Group B with Belgium, Sweden and Turkey. Their first match took place at GelreDome in Arnhem against the Turks on 11 June 2000 with Italy taking the honours 2-1. Antonio Conte opened the scoring in the second half before Okan Buruk equalised to set up an interesting last half-hour. The match was settled with 20 minutes to go when Italy were awarded a penalty which was converted by Filippo Inzaghi. Maximum points were also collected in the following match as Italy upset co-hosts Belgium in Brussels with a 2-0 victory. A Francesco Totti header from a set piece in the sixth minute and a beautiful strike from just outside the penalty area from Stefano Fiore in the second half settled matters in favour of the Italians.

They secured another victory in the final group match (and with it the top spot), beating Sweden 2-1. Luigi Di Biagio scored the first goal with a decisive header from a corner before Henrik Larsson restored parity with 13 minutes remaining. A mistake in the Swedish defence was then capitalised upon by Alessandro Del Piero, who ran with the ball before unleashing a superb shot into the net to ensure a third consecutive victory for his nation.

The quarter-final clash took place in Brussels and the opponents were Romania. Italy took the lead just after the half-hour mark when Francesco Totti chested the ball beautifully before skilfully placing it into the net. A second goal just before half-time put the Italians in total control when Filippo Inzaghi broke free before slotting home. There were no further goals, so Italy were now in the last four of the competition.

Italy had already beaten one of the co-hosts and now did the same to Holland to reach their second final in the Euros. The game was played at the Amsterdam Arena and went to penalties. The story of the match was possession and chances (which were at a premium) for the Dutch, but the Italian defence stood firm and was superbly marshalled by Fabio Cannavaro. The best chance of the game fell to Holland when they were awarded a second-half penalty but there was an Italian reprieve when Patrick Kluivert's shot hit the post and not the net. There was more orange heartache from the spot in the shoot-out with Italy winning 3-1 with three out of four spot kicks not converted by the home nation. The scorers for Italy were Luigi Di Biagio, Gianluca Pessotto and Francesco Totti.

The final was played on 2 July 2000 at De Kuip in Rotterdam between Italy and France. Both nations had won the competition once before, so the chance to add another trophy was tantalisingly close.

It was almost first blood to France as early as the fifth minute when a half-volley from Thierry Henry hit the post. Despite this, chances in the first half were at a premium and it ended without a goal being scored. This changed in the 55th minute when Italy took the lead. A smart move between Totti and Pessotto ended with the latter crossing the ball which beat both Laurent Blanc and Marcel Desailly, allowing Marco Delvecchio to score from close range.

Now was the moment for the French to try to take control and press for the equaliser. The Italian defence once more stood firm, answering the questions that the French posed. Then in the third minute of stoppage time, France's goalkeeper Fabien Barthez took a long free kick. The ball reached the head of David Trezeguet, who was then able to find Sylvain Wiltord. The Frenchman controlled the ball with his chest before firing a shot through Alessandro Nesta's legs and then past Francesco Toldo in the Italian goal to make the game all-square.

Italy were shell-shocked and needed to regroup as the match went into extra time with a golden goal at stake. The impetus was with the French as the first half of extra time commenced, and the match was settled just moments before the end of the first period.

Demetrio Albertini had played some decisive passes during the finals but this time he mis-controlled one. This allowed Robert Pires to take the ball and cross into the Italian box, where he found Trezeguet. He had played an instrumental part in his nation's equaliser, and it was his half-volley into the top corner that gave them the winning goal. Italy had been so close to winning the match in normal time but now found themselves on the receiving end of a golden goal that gave their opponents the victory. Just like four years previously, in 1996, when the Germans had defeated the Czechs in the same manner.

Dino Zoff's team had played well during the whole tournament and could consider themselves unlucky to be on the losing side. In contrast, France were now European and World Champions.

It would not be the last time that these two great footballing nations would meet in a final in the first decade of the new century.

2004

Manager: Giovanni Trapattoni

The finals were held in Portugal and in the qualifying competition to reach the promised land, Italy were placed in Group 9 with Wales, Yugoslavia, Finland and Azerbaijan. Just like in the qualifying rounds four years previously, Italy finished top of the group with their biggest winning margins being two 4-0 victories. On the receiving end were Azerbaijan and, just as in the previous campaign, Wales. This time, though, Wales were afforded revenge with a 2-1 home victory. It was Italy's only defeat of the campaign as they won five matches and drew the other two, 1-1. The first one was against Yugoslavia in Naples in October 2002 and by the time that the return leg was played almost a year later, Yugoslavia had become Serbia and Montenegro. Italy finished the group on 17 points and by scoring the same number of goals with only four conceded. Filippo Inzaghi was leading scorer with six goals with Alessandro Del Piero finishing with just one less. Denmark, Italy, Sweden and Bulgaria were the four teams that made up Group C for the finals.

Despite not being beaten in the qualifying group, Italy were eliminated at this stage in the finals, finishing in third place behind Sweden and Denmark. All three nations finished on five points with Sweden having a better goal difference, courtesy of a 5-0 victory over Bulgaria. In fact, it was the victories over the Bulgarians that determined the final placings. Denmark beat them 2-0 and Italy could only manage a 2-1 victory. All the other games were draws.

Italy's first game had been against Sweden which finished goalless, followed by a 1-1 score against the Danes, Simone Perrotta bagging the goal. The final group game was the 2-1 victory over Bulgaria. A Martin Petrov penalty on the stroke of half-time gave the Bulgarians the lead, which was cancelled out with second-half goals from Perrotta and a last-minute winner from Antonio Cassano which ensured Italian victory, but was not enough to see any further progression. The champions were Greece, who defied the odds to beat Portugal in the final.

2008
Manager: Roberto Donadoni

Roberto Donadoni had come through the ranks for his nation with flying colours, initially with the under-21 side that reached the final of the European Championship in 1986. This was followed up with senior appearances in the 1988 and 1996 Euros and the World Cups in 1990 and 1994. Donadoni could play anywhere in midfield, except maybe in a defensive role. He could play on either wing, in the centre or in an attacking position. His contribution to the Italian cause was very significant during these years, with his pace, agility and technical ability at the forefront.

Donadoni was given the Italian job just days after Marcello Lippi had stepped down, with the nation recently crowned World Champions, in 2006. His sights were set firmly on taking Italy further and making them European Champions as well.

Italy were paired with no fewer than six other nations in their qualifying group to reach the 2008 finals, which were co-hosted by Austria and Switzerland. Group B also included France, Scotland, Ukraine, Lithuania, Georgia and the Faroe Islands. This meant that each nation would have to play 12 matches.

Italy's campaign started badly with just one point in the first two games: a 1-1 draw in Naples against Lithuania was followed up with a 3-1 loss to rivals France at the Stade de France. However, nine wins and a draw from the remaining games completely turned the tide in Italy's favour, beginning with a 2-0 home victory in Rome against Ukraine, with goals from Massimo Oddo (penalty) and Luca Toni making the difference. This was followed up with a 3-1 victory away in Georgia and from that moment on, the Azzurri never looked back. The only points dropped were at home to France where no goals were scored.

Two nations would qualify from the group and the smart money was on both the Italians and the French. Sure enough, Italy and France secured qualification to the finals on 17 November 2007 following Italy's 2-1 win against Scotland, after France had beaten Lithuania in the previous month. They became the fifth and sixth teams in the whole of the qualification process to book their places. It was Italy who came out on top, securing 29 points out of 36, as opposed to France who finished on 26. Italy scored 22 goals and conceded just nine in the campaign. Luca Toni was top scorer with five goals.

The clashes between Italy and France continued in the finals as they were both drawn to play in Group C alongside Holland and Romania. Italy's first match was against Holland in Bern (Switzerland) on 9 June 2008. It was a disastrous start for Italy as the Dutch were rampant, winning the game 3-0 with Ruud van Nistelrooy, Wesley Sneijder and Giovanni van Bronckhorst scoring. The Dutch had played superbly and qualification from the group stages was confirmed in their next match against France as they ran out big winners once more, 4-1. Italy's second match was played in Zürich against Romania and it finished all square at 1-1. The game sprang to life in two second-half minutes with Romania taking the lead on 55 minutes through Adrian Mutu, then Italy levelling just a minute later when Christian Panucci touched the ball home following up from Giorgio Chiellini's header across goal. It could have got so much worse for Italy when Romania were awarded a penalty late on when Panucci dragged down Daniel Niculae. A Romanian goal at such a late stage would have surely consigned Italy to going home after their third match, but Gianluigi Buffon's save from Mutu breathed life back into the Azzurri and the passage out of the group was secured with a 2-0 victory over France in a match once more played at the Letzigrund in Zürich. Italy were awarded a penalty in the 25th minute which was converted by Andrea Pirlo and victory was confirmed in the second half when a 30-yard free kick taken by Daniele De Rossi was deflected off Thierry Henry. Italy's hold over the French had continued after successes at the World Cup two years previous and in the qualifying group to reach Austria and Switzerland.

Italy then faced Spain in the quarter-final, which was played in Vienna on 22 June. The match did not live up to expectations, with the game goalless after 120 minutes of turgid play with chances few and far between. So, the tie had to be decided on penalties. Amazingly, this was Spain's fourth attempt to navigate a quarter-final penalty shoot-out, and they had lost the other three. The previous matches had been in the World Cups of 1986 and 2002 and Euro '96, so the omens were not looking good for the Spanish as David Villa stepped up to take the first kick. However, it would prove to be fourth time lucky as he scored, then Spain keeper Iker Casillas became the hero, saving from Daniele De Rossi and Antonio Di Natale. Italy had a reprieve when Daniel Guiza saw his spot kick saved by Buffon, but Arsenal's Cesc Fabregas slid home the crucial penalty to finally lay the 22 June quarter-final ghost to rest for the Spanish at the expense of Italy, winning the shoot-out 4-2. Italy were back on the plane home and Spain went on to win the competition for the first time with a 1-0 victory in the final against Germany in Vienna.

2012
Manager: Cesare Prandelli
The early Euro finals of the 21st century had witnessed countries collaborating in hosting them and 2012 was no exception, with duties shared between Poland and Ukraine. For the group qualification, Italy were placed into Group C and would play home and away against

Estonia, Serbia, Slovenia, Northern Ireland and the Faroe Islands. The bookies made Italy firm favourites to qualify, and this was achieved at a canter with them winning the group by the considerable margin of ten points over their nearest rivals, Estonia. The Azzurri won eight and drew the other two matches to finish on 26 points. Their goal difference was plus 18 with only two goals conceded, both away from Italian soil, in a 2-1 victory against Estonia and 1-1 draw with Serbia. The other match that finished all-square was against Northern Ireland in Belfast. This meant that all matches played in Italy were victories without any goals conceded. Italy recorded 3-0 wins against Estonia and Northern Ireland and were also awarded a 3-0 victory against Serbia when the game was abandoned due to crowd trouble after just six minutes in October 2010. The biggest win was 5-0 against the Faroe Islands and the other three points were collected from Slovenia, 1-0. Antonio Cassano topped the goal-scoring charts with six goals to his name with a plethora of players also contributing to the cause.

For the finals themselves, Italy were paired with Spain, the Republic of Ireland and Croatia. It was widely anticipated that Spain and Italy would progress to the knockout rounds and this is precisely what happened. The first match was between those two giants of international football and was played on 10 June 2012 with the game finishing 1-1 and both goals were scored in the second half, just minutes apart. Italy were technically astute and had several good chances to take the lead in the first period with Spain's keeper, Iker Casillas, in fine form. The deadlock was broken just after the hour mark when Pirlo took the ball past Xavi before expertly playing a cleverly weighted pass to Antonio Di Natale, who in turn took the ball past Gerard Pique and Sergio Ramos before calmly stroking a curling shot beyond the advancing Casillas. Spain were back on level terms just three minutes later through a smart goal from Cesc Fabregas after he was played in by David Villa.

The second game in the group presented a similar scenario when Italy took on Croatia. This time, the Italians led through a goal scored by Pirlo in the first half. The equaliser came in the second period through Mario Mandžukić. Italy's third and final game was against the Republic of Ireland, and it was a game that the Azzurri had to win to guarantee progression, while hoping that Spain took care of matters against Croatia. The Spanish ensured they played their part with a 1-0 victory, whilst Italy beat their opponents 2-0, Antonio Cassano and Mario Balotelli netting.

The quarter-final draw saw Italy take on England in Kyiv. It was an intriguing match that went to penalties. Over the period of the 120 minutes, Italy were much the better team as outlined by Jürgen Klinsmann who was a pundit on the BBC's match coverage: 'Italy were far superior to England. What impressed me was technically they controlled the game, but also, they were physically stronger. That surprised me, and they deserved to get into the semis where they will expect a good clash with

Germany. I had hopes for England but to be honest they didn't deserve it because they could not keep tempo with Italy, they didn't close down spaces and it was too big a mountain to climb.'

Italy won the penalty shoot-out 4-2 with Balotelli, Pirlo, Antonio Nocerino and Alessandro Diamanti all scoring. The only player not to put the ball into the net successfully was Riccardo Montolivo.

The semi-final against Germany took place on 28 June and was played at the National Stadium in Warsaw in front of a crowd of 55,540. Italy were in electric form as the game kicked off and found themselves two goals to the good by the 36th minute with both goals being scored by Mario Balotelli, who was simply unstoppable. Balotelli put his country in front when he directed Antonio Cassano's cross past Germany keeper Manuel Neuer, before adding his second with a telling strike from Montolivo's pass. The score stayed the same until deep into stoppage time when Mesut Özil converted a penalty, but it was much too late in the game for Germany to make a comeback they frankly did not deserve.

The final against Spain was played on the first day of July at the Olimpiyskiy National Sports Complex in Kyiv in front of millions watching across the world and 63,170 in attendance at the stadium. Spain had knocked out Italy on penalties on the way to winning the previous tournament and both teams had played each other in the first group game of 2012, thus, it was expected to be a fiercely contested match. However, it was a one-sided final with Spain winning 4-0. This is how the BBC reported on the game:

> 'Spain made history in magical fashion as they outclassed Italy and claimed a successive European crown to add to their 2010 World Cup triumph. Vicente Del Bosque's side staged a compelling claim to be the greatest international side of all time as the Euro 2012 final was transformed into an exhibition with Italy – who performed creditably for long periods – passed brutally into submission. David Silva's header was reward for Spain's early supremacy and new Barcelona recruit Jordi Alba doubled the lead just before half-time with a blistering run and finish.'

Phil McNulty's report continued:

> 'The scoreline was emphatic at the conclusion but Italy performed with great resolve. Once they were reduced to ten men after losing third substitute Thiago Motta to injury, however, they were ruthlessly exposed by masters of the passing art. Fernando Torres emerged as a late substitute to make a powerful impact: steering home Spain's third then setting up Chelsea team-mate Juan Mata to inflict the final wound on a bedraggled Italy.'

Italy were shell-shocked to their core. Spain were double European Champions whilst also World Champions, to cap an exceptional period of success for Vicente Del Bosque's band of Spanish brothers.

2016
Manager: Antonio Conte

All roads led to France in qualifying for the 2016 finals with Antonio Conte in the hot seat. Conte had taken over from Cesare Prandelli after the World Cup debacle in 2014. His contract was for two years, which ensured he would oversee qualification for France. Italy were paired with Croatia, Norway, Bulgaria, Azerbaijan and Malta in the group stages.

Once more, Italy topped the group after the ten games, finishing on 24 points, which was four more than their nearest rivals, Croatia. It would have been just three points, but Croatia were deducted one point after racist chants in their match against Italy. For the second successive qualifying campaign, Italy prospered without losing a game. This time it was seven wins and three draws and the leading goalscorer was Graziano Pellè, who contributed three of his country's 16 goals scored in qualification.

Just a few months before the actual finals, the *Federazione Italiana Giuoco Calcio* (FIGC) confirmed Conte would step down as manager after Euro 2016. This did not come as a shock as the tactics that Conte used were uninspiring, as was his squad selection for the finals in which they were drawn against Belgium, the Republic of Ireland and Sweden in Group E.

For the first time ever in the competition, the European Championship was contested by 24 teams, having been expanded from the 16-team format used since 1996. Under the new format, the finalists played a group stage consisting of six groups of four teams. This was then followed by a knockout phase including three rounds and the final.

The top two from each group went through, plus the four best third-placed teams, and Italy did not have to worry about being one of them as they finished top of the group with two wins and a draw. They opened their campaign with a 2-0 victory against Belgium at the Parc Olympique Lyonnais, Emanuele Giaccherini scoring in the first half before a last-minute goal from Pellè settled matters. This victory was followed up with a 1-0 win over Sweden in Toulouse on 17 June 2016, Éder netting to put his country through to the knockout stages. The criticism of Conte's tactics and selection had somewhat dissipated by now. It was not to be a 100 per cent winning start though, as in game three an 85th-minute goal from Robbie Brady earned Ireland a famous victory. Italy still topped the group with Belgium and the Republic of Ireland also progressing.

Revenge was a dish best served cold for the Italians in the round of 16, with a 2-0 victory against Spain. Giorgio Chiellini scored the game's opening goal in the 33rd minute, bundling the ball into the net from close range after David de Gea had parried an Éder free kick in wet conditions in the first half. The victory was secured in injury time when Pellè volleyed the ball in from close range. In truth though, victory should have been secured well before the dying minutes of the game with De Gea making outstanding saves during the match.

The quarter-final was played in Bordeaux on 2 July and the opponents were Germany, who had not conceded a goal in the first four matches of the tournament and looked the better team in the opening exchanges of the game. They were denied the lead on 15 minutes when Bastian Schweinsteiger had a goal quite rightly struck off for a clear push on Mattia De Sciglio. There were also chances for Mario Gomez and Thomas Muller, but it was Italy who had the best chance when Stefano Sturaro's effort was deflected narrowly wide by Jérôme Boateng.

The second half continued in the same manner with Germany on the front foot and they very nearly had the lead when Thomas Muller had a shot acrobatically cleared by Alessandro Florenzi just after the interval. However, Germany's persistence eventually paid off in the 65th minute when Mesut Özil scored with a half-volley just after the ball had deflected off Leonardo Bonucci. It could have been two for Germany shortly after when a Mario Gomez back-heel was superbly saved by Buffon. Bonucci may have been unlucky with a deflection that had given the Germans the lead, but it was his penalty that brought Italy back into the game with 13 minutes remaining after a handball decision went against Boateng.

There were no more goals scored in the remainder of the match and extra time, and so it was on to penalties to decide the outcome.

The first ten penalties saw three missed by both nations and at 2-2 the shoot-out entered its sudden death phase. Emanuele Giaccherini, Marco Parolo, De Sciglio, Hummels, Joshua Kimmich and Boateng all put their spot kicks away before Neuer saved Matteo Darmian's low penalty to his left. Italy were devastated as Germany celebrated.

Both managers were in philosophical mood after the match. Conte said, 'I want to thank the boys. They were extraordinary for two years for me. They topped it off with this special experience. I'm sorry because they deserved to go through. We made the fans proud of us, and we made the players truly aware that it's a privilege to wear the shirt.'

Meanwhile, Germany manager Joachim Löw said, 'It was a drama – extra time and with two sides on the highest tactical level. The penalties missed were even more dramatic. We were lucky. There is nothing I could blame the team for. We were the better team in the 120 minutes.'

Conte had won over his detractors somewhat as the tournament progressed before packing his bags to take over the hot seat at Chelsea. Germany failed to win their semi-final match against France, who in turn finished as runners-up to Portugal. The score in the final was 1-0 after extra time.

Italy had been in two finals since the turn of the new century and lost both of them. These defeats had hurt the nation and they set about trying to put things right for the next competition, scheduled for the summer of 2020. Little did they, or anyone, know that Euro 2020 would be postponed and played exactly a year later instead in the most extraordinary of circumstances.

FIFA World Cup Qualifying Campaign: 2018

Host nation for the finals: Russia
Qualifying group: UEFA Group G
Opponents: Spain, Albania, Israel, Macedonia,
Liechtenstein
Manager: Gian Piero Ventura

ITALY'S FIRST match in the qualifying group for the 2018 World Cup was against Israel and it was played at the Sammy Ofer Stadium in Haifa on 5 September 2016. It was Gian Piero Ventura's first competitive match in charge of Italy since taking over from Antonio Conte just a few weeks before.

Ventura was able to welcome back Leonardo Bonucci after he had missed a friendly against France just days before, for personal reasons.

It was important to hit the ground running, as only the group winners would have a guaranteed place in the finals, and Italy went in front and signalled clear intentions after just 14 minutes of the match. The ball was played to Luca Antonelli, who found himself in clear territory on the left before sending the ball across for Graziano Pellè, who arrived in perfect time to meet it and scored from close range. Italy were then awarded a penalty on the half-hour mark, and this was converted by Antonio Candreva, who neatly found the bottom-right corner with Israel's shot-stopper David Goresh sent the wrong way.

Just four minutes later, the hosts were back in the game. It was a goal of pure quality, as Ben Haim seized upon the opportunity to chip the ball into the far top corner, leaving Gianluigi Buffon stranded. There were no further first-half goals although a header from Éder on the stroke of half-time almost restored Italy's two-goal lead. It was firmly goalbound before Goresh made a great save, tipping the ball round the post.

This seemed to spur the hosts on, as the second half began with a long-range effort from Nir Bitton parried away by Buffon. In the 55th minute Italy were down to ten men when Giorgio Chiellini received his marching orders for two yellow cards, with the second one coming because of a foul on Tomer Hemed. Replays showed the rugged defender was unlucky as the incident looked more like a collision rather than one with any intention of malice on the side of Chiellini, who was making his 90th appearance for his country. This forced the Italians to regroup, and this was done successfully as they were quick to close Israel down, restricting them to long-range efforts struck more in hope than anything else. The match was over as a contest in the 83rd minute when substitute Ciro Immobile was able to get the better of his defender before producing a fine low shot into the far corner, and Italy won 3-1.

Italy's next match was a much sterner test as they hosted Spain one month later in Turin. There were no goals scored in the first half, which really was a compliment to the Italian defence, with Spain having almost 73 per cent possession.

The pressure turned into a goal in the 55th minute when Buffon missed an attempted clearance, leaving Vitolo with the simplest of tap-ins. It was no more than the Spaniards deserved, with Italy's fir power nowhere to be seen – that was until the 82nd minute, when they were awarded a penalty after Éder had been tripped by Sergio Ramos. Up stepped De Rossi who made no mistake and levelled the match at 1-1, which is how it stayed.

That extended Italy's unbeaten run in World Cup and Euros qualifying campaigns, which stretched back to 2006, when they had been defeated 3-1 by France.

Both Spain and Italy had four points after the opening two games, although neither topped the group, as the top spot was held by Albania, who beat Liechtenstein 2-0 to maintain their 100 per cent winning start.

There was no time to dwell on the draw with Spain, as three days later, on 9 October, the Azzurri were away to Macedonia for match three of the campaign. Italy came away with a victory. They took the lead in the 24th minute courtesy of a goal scored by Andrea Belotti. They had made a shaky start to the match but held on to go into the break with the lead. Many expected Italy to impose their authority in the second half, but the Macedonian players did not receive the memo. In the 57th minute they were level after Italy had lost the ball in the middle of the park, with Ilija Nestorovski taking advantage to score. Just two minutes later, Macedonia were celebrating taking the lead when another mistake in midfield allowed Feran Hasani to pounce. There now looked to be only one winner as Macedonia pushed forward to potentially cement a famous victory. However, two goals in the final 15 minutes from Ciro Immobile broke the host nation's hearts as Italy breathed a sigh of relief, winning the match 3-2.

The win lifted Italy into second place (on goal difference) behind Spain, who had beaten Albania away, 2-0, ending the hosts' 100 per cent record.

A third consecutive away victory (and the last game of 2016) took place at Rheinpark Stadion in Vaduz on 12 November. This was the national stadium of Liechtenstein, and the attendance was just shy of 6,000. Ventura made tactical changes for this match as he deployed a 4-2-4 formation, and it was a decision that bore fruit in a ruthless first half which saw Italy score four goals. Italy were in front on 11 minutes when Belotti fired home from close range to set the scene. The lead was doubled moments later when Belotti turned provider to allow Immobile to score. Antonio Candreva added a third before Belotti made it two for himself, and four for his country, when he collected a chipped pass from Giacomo Bonaventura and drilled it past Peter Jehle.

Italy continued to dominate in the second half and could have extended their lead further, with Immobile going close with a header before De Rossi fired wide. There was a scare for Italy when Buffon (who was making his 166th senior international appearance) had to be quick off the mark and rush from his line to clear the ball with Liechtenstein forward Dennis Salanovic in a menacing position following a mistake in the Italian defence. Italy could not add to their first-half tally, despite having late chances when Belotti sent a glancing header just wide and Simone Zaza was denied at close range.

Italy finished the 2016 leg of qualification with ten points, which put them level with Spain, who topped the group with a far superior goal difference. Still, it had been a solid start for Ventura.

Their first game of 2017 saw Italy back on home soil against Albania with the match being played in Palmero on 24 March. Italy won 2-0, but the occasion was marred when the game was held up for nearly ten minutes due to visiting fans throwing flares and smoke bombs on to the pitch. Italy were awarded a penalty in the 12th minute, which was initially delayed due to the antics taking place on the terraces. Daniele De Rossi kept his counsel and duly slotted the ball into the net. Immobile headed home late in the second half to leave Italy second in Group G, still behind free-scoring Spain, who took care of Israel on home soil, 4-1.

It was down to Italy to run with the 'free-scoring' baton in the next round of matches, on 11 June, as they hosted Liechtenstein in Udine. The final scoreline was 5-0 but that didn't do justice to Italy's superiority in the 90 minutes, the hosts having 37 efforts on the Liechtenstein goal. Despite the dominance, it took Italy 35 minutes to open the scoring and the goal came from Lorenzo Insigne, who superbly trapped the ball with his chest before firing home. Insigne then turned provider to find Belotti to make it 2-0. The remaining goals came from Éder, who volleyed in the third with 15 minutes remaining, a long-range shot from substitute Federico Bernardeschi, and Manolo Gabbiadini, who rounded off the scoring in the 91st minute.

It may have seemed a lifetime between the second and third goals, but the win was a convincing one in the end, with Gianluigi Buffon not having to make a single save.

Spain's 2-1 victory in Macedonia kept them on top of the group after six matches but only on goal difference, Spain having scored 18 goals to Italy's 14 with both nations on 16 points. With only one nation guaranteed to progress to the finals, it was becoming more and more obvious that the crunch match to decide who would come out on top would be in the next round, on 2 September, when Spain would be hosting Italy.

The game was played at the Bernabéu Stadium in Madrid. Before the match, Spain's Isco had only scored three goals for his country and by the end of it, he had almost doubled his tally as Spain ran rampant against

Italy, who were second-best all evening. The Real Madrid playmaker was on home soil, and it showed as early as the 13th minute when he curled the ball into the Italian net from a free kick. The same player then doubled the lead moments before half-time to give Italy a mountain to climb. The only goal of the second half came from Álvaro Morata, who was able to convert after assistance from Sergio Ramos.

Spain's 3-0 victory now opened up a three-point gap over Italy, with an improved goal difference of ten over their nearest rivals. Ventura had stuck with the 4-2-4 formation which had served him well against teams that were not as well developed, but this was Spain they were playing, and they had returned to their sumptuous best and looked strong in pole position. There would be no room for error when Italy hosted Israel just three days after the mauling at the hands of Spain.

As expected, Italy dominated possession in Reggio Emilia with Israel's defence standing firm against the blue tide that attacked them. Italy were missing their regular centre-back pairing of Chiellini, who was out injured, and Bonucci, who was suspended. There was nearly a third senior omission in the early stages of the match when Buffon collided with Davide Astori, but despite taking a knock to the head, he was deemed fit to carry on, much to the delight of Ventura and his backroom staff.

Israel came very close to taking the lead through Marwan Kabha, but he was challenged by Andrea

Conti, who did enough to thwart him. Both nations went into the half-time break without having been able to penetrate but all this changed eight minutes into the second half when a cross from Antonio Candreva was met by the head of Immobile, who powered the ball into the net.

It may not have been pretty, but the 1-0 win was still an important one and kept Italy three points off Spain, whose goal difference was further increased with an 8-0 win in Liechtenstein.

If the 3-0 defeat in Spain had derailed Italy, then the next match at home against Macedonia firmly put the nails in the coffin of finishing in top place and claiming automatic qualification. A 1-1 draw against Macedonia coupled with Spain's 3-0 victory against Albania confirmed that Italy would have to qualify via the play-offs.

The last two group matches were played on 6 October, with Giorgio Chiellini putting Italy in front on 40 minutes. By that time, Spain had scored all three of their goals, making Italy's result irrelevant to the outcome of the group. Macedonia's equaliser came in the 77th minute, courtesy of Aleksandar Trajkovski.

The tenth and final games of the campaign took place three days later with Italy and Spain both collecting 1-0 away wins. Italy's win was in Albania and the goal was scored by Candreva.

2018 FIFA World Cup qualification – UEFA Group G Final Table

Pos	Team	Pld	W	D	L	GF	GA	GD	Pts
1	Spain	10	9	1	0	36	3	33	28
2	Italy	10	7	2	1	21	8	13	23
3	Albania	10	4	1	5	10	13	-3	13
4	Israel	10	4	0	6	10	15	-5	12
5	Macedonia	10	3	2	5	15	15	0	11
6	Liechtenstein	10	0	0	10	1	39	-38	0

The qualification play-offs would be contested by the best eight runners-up from the initial groups. The eight European nations involved were Switzerland, Italy, Denmark, Croatia, Sweden, Northern Ireland, Greece and the Republic of Ireland. The countries were split into two pots, A and B, for the draw for the two-legged play-offs. Pot A contained the best-placed runners-up: Italy, Switzerland, Denmark and Croatia. The 'non-seeded' countries in Pot B were Northern Ireland, Sweden, the Republic of Ireland and Greece. The draw was made on 17 October in Zurich with the following matches to be played on a home and away basis between 9 and 14 November 2017:

> Switzerland v Northern Ireland
> Croatia v Greece
> Denmark v Republic of Ireland
> Italy v Sweden

Italy's first leg took place at the Friends' Arena in Solna, Sweden, on 10 November. The early exchanges of the match centred around the physical facets with Leonardo Bonucci receiving an elbow from Ola Toivonen, which left the AC Milan defender writhing in pain. Chances were few and far between, with the best falling to Emil Forsberg for Sweden when he fired a free kick over the crossbar. Italy's biggest threat came from a header from Andrea Belotti, but in truth it was a weak effort.

Sweden almost took the lead just before the half-time break when Marcus Berg capitalised on hesitation from Giorgio Chiellini, but Buffon was able to clear the ball before any real damage could be done.

However, there was a different outcome just after the hour mark when Sweden's Jakob Johansson struck the ball inside the Italian penalty area. A slight deflection off De Rossi took his shot past Buffon and into the net to give the Swedes the lead.

Italy enjoyed plenty of possession from that moment and came close to equalising, but full-back Matteo Darmian was unlucky when his long-range effort hit the post. The match ended 1-0 in favour of Sweden and Ventura was in a philosophical mood afterwards: 'We just need to get a result now. We need to overturn it all in Milan. San Siro has to take us by the hand, and we must put in a great performance for the crowd. Considering what happened on the pitch, the result was harsh. I hope that in Milan we get given what they were given tonight. In such an important match, a different approach was needed.'

The return leg was played just three days later at the San Siro in Milan, with the vast majority of the near 73,000 fans in the stadium optimistic that Italy would overturn the 1-0 deficit. It had been 60 years since the Azzurri had not qualified for the World Cup finals.

The Swedish team came into the second leg with a clearly defined game plan. During the whole of the 90 minutes that followed, Italy had 76 per cent possession and 20 attempts on goal. Ciro Immobile was very much in the midst of these chances with his best effort coming in the first half when a low drive was cleared off the line by Andreas Granqvist. The Swede played a major part in Italy's downfall alongside his defensive team-mates who sat deep, clearing their lines with consummate professionalism. At the end of the match, the stats showed that the Swedes had made more than 50 clearances as well as numerous interceptions.

Both nations had claims for penalty awards. A rash challenge from Ludwig Augustinsson on Marco Paralo was not taken any further and Italy were fortunate themselves to get away with a couple of handballs in their own penalty area with both Matteo Darmian and Andrea Barzagli involved. Sweden's goalkeeper was also in fine form, with Robin Olsen superbly marshalling his defence whilst making important saves from Jorginho and Alessandro Florenzi. At the final whistle, many of the Italy players simply fell to the ground whilst others were reduced to tears. For Sweden, though, it was a job well done as they hugged and celebrated knowing that their place in the following summer's World Cup was now assured, alongside Switzerland, Croatia and Denmark, who had also been victorious over their two legs.

The 1-0 aggregate win for Sweden was not the way that Gianluigi Buffon had envisaged bowing out after 175 appearances for his nation. He faced the cameras at the end of the match and said, 'I'm not sorry for myself but all of Italian football. We failed at something which also means something on a social level. There's regret at finishing like that, not because time passes. Those who've played know how hard these matches are. We weren't able to express ourselves at our best. We lacked the composure to score. Play-offs are decided by episodes, and they went against us, but you can understand that when you're at fault.'

Buffon was full of admiration for his fellow team members and for the future of the Italian national side, 'We have pride, strength and we're stubborn. We know how to get back up again as we've always done. I'm leaving an Italy side that will know how to speak for itself. Hugs to everyone, especially those I've shared this wonderful journey with.'

Although it was reported that Ventura declined to be interviewed on Italian TV straight after the match, he did make comments in the aftermath. 'I apologise to Italians for this result. It's horrible to see a World Cup without Italy, but it's done now, and I can't do anything about it.'

Ventura was also pressed on his overall record in charge of national affairs. 'My record is one of the best of the last 40 years. I lost only two games in two years.'

Croatia may have qualified for the finals at the second attempt, but their momentum carried them forward and they finished in second place, losing to France 4-2 in the final on 15 July at the Luzhniki Stadium in Moscow. For France, it had been exactly 20 years since their previous victory, and they were World Champions for the second time.

UEFA European Championship Campaign: 2020

Host nations for the finals: Azerbaijan, Denmark, England, Germany, Hungary, Italy, Netherlands, Romania, Russia, Scotland, Spain

Qualifying group: UEFA Group J
Opponents: Finland, Greece, Bosnia and Herzegovina, Armenia, Liechtenstein
Manager: Roberto Mancini

TO MARK the 60th anniversary of the European Championship, UEFA president Michel Platini announced that several nations would host matches in the finals and it would be a truly 'pan-European' showpiece, as opposed to a single or co-hosted tournament. The finals themselves were scheduled to be played between 12 June and 12 July 2020. However, it would take a further 12 months for them to take place.

There was no automatic qualification for any of the 55 nations that competed for the 24 places on offer. Italy were placed in Group J and by the end of the campaign, it was the perfect ten for them.

Italy's first match was against Finland, in Udine on 23 March 2019. Finland's tactics centred around trying to frustrate the hosts but it didn't stop them going a goal down within the first ten minutes, when an attempted clearance went straight to Nicolò Barella, who was able to hit the ball first time from the edge of the area and watch as it sailed into the net after taking a deflection which wrong-footed Lukas Hradecky. There were no further goals in the first half, although Italy's Federico Bernardeschi did have a penalty appeal turned down.

Italy were looking for that killer second goal as the second half commenced, but it was very nearly all square when Robin Lod's advancement down the right-hand side saw him feed the ball through to the dangerous Teemu Pukki, but to the relief of the Italians, his shot went wide. This was the wake-up call that Italy needed, as they stretched their lead with just 15 minutes remaining. Ciro Immobile was able to thread the ball to Moise Kean, and the 19-year-old (in only his second international appearance) duly slotted it past Hradecky to double his country's lead to 2-0 and ensure a solid start was made to the campaign.

Italy's next match came just three days later against Liechtenstein in Parma. Once again, the game plan was to nullify Italian attacks as much as possible but this idea was well and truly derailed as the hosts scored four times in the first half. The breakthrough came on 17 minutes via the head of Stefano Sensi following a cross from Leonardo Spinazzola, and 15 minutes later the tally was doubled when Marco Verratti's sublime curling effort found the back of the net. Italy were then awarded two penalties which were successfully converted by Fabio Quagliarella. Finland went down to ten men as a result of the second penalty.

The game was effectively over as a spectacle and Italy were able to add two more goals in the second period to run out 6-0 winners. Kean's impact in the early stages of the competition was once more felt with 20 minutes remaining, courtesy of a header, before Leonardo Pavoletti wrapped up proceedings, tapping in from close range.

Italy's next two matches took place in June and also brought maximum points, albeit by smaller margins. First up was a trip to the Olympic Stadium in Athens where the opponents were Greece. Once more the match was effectively over in the first half with Italy taking a strong 3-0 lead into the break. Nicolò Barella opened the scoring after Andrea Belotti had assisted with a smart pull-back. Moments later, Italy doubled their lead courtesy of a beautiful curling finish from Lorenzo Insigne before Leonardo Bonucci made it 3-0 with a header. There were no goals in the second period as Italy sat back to protect their lead. The closest the hosts came was a half-volley from Kostas Fortounis which was palmed away by Salvatore Sirigu. Italy's best chance fell to Federico Chiesa, who fired over after he had found himself unmarked at close range.

A fourth straight victory was recorded back on home soil in Turin just a few days later, against Bosnia and

Herzegovina, although it was the first match in which Italy conceded. From the off, Italy's opponents took the game to their hosts with some clever counter-attacking, and it was no surprise when they took the lead. A back-heel from Muhamed Bešić allowed Edin Višća to venture down the right before finding Edin Džeko, who put his country one up just after the half-hour mark.

Italy's best chance in the first period fell to Quagliarella, who was denied by a fine save from Ibrahim Šehić. Italy were level soon after the break when Lorenzo Insigne fired in a stunning volley from the edge of the area. Now it was down to Italy to break down Bosnia and make it four consecutive victories. This happened in the 86th minute when Marco Verratti found himself with space and time to fire in the winner.

The victory may not have been as convincing as previous ones, but Roberto Mancini was just as happy, as he expressed in one of his post-match interviews: 'The lads gave their all. It wasn't easy to turn a match like this around, we risked a bit on counter-attacks, but we clearly dominated in the second half.' Mancini was critical of some of his team's earlier play though. 'We took too many risks in the first half but then we improved.'

Not surprisingly, Italy found themselves top of Group J with a maximum 12 points, three more than Finland who occupied second place.

September brought no respite for the teams vying with the Azzurri, with two further matches against Armenia and Finland on foreign soil. For the second

Held in high esteem! *Vittorio Pozzo is proudly held high by his players after winning the 1934 World Cup*

There's a Starman! *Giuseppe Meazza was one of the first Italian greats who played mainly for Inter Milan and sparkled for his country in the glorious 1930s*

In Memoriam. *Memorial to the 'Grande Torino' football team killed when their plane crashed into the hill below the Basilica di Superga in 1949*

One of the greatest games ever! *Action from the World Cup semi-final in Mexico 1970. Italy 4 West Germany 3*

One of the greatest goal celebrations! *Marco Tardelli after scoring in the World Cup Final against West Germany in 1982*

The Agony! Roberto Baggio stands alone after missing his penalty in the shoot-out in the World Cup Final against Brazil in 1994

The Ecstasy! Fabio Cannavaro lifts the World Cup in 2006

Italy do not qualify for 2018! Sweden celebrate their win in the 2018 play-off match that took them to the World Cup finals in Russia

Italy do not qualify for 2022! North Macedonia celebrate their win in the 2022 play-off match that took them to the World Cup finals in 2022

Well done!
Roberto Mancini is congratulated after guiding his team to 2020 Euro glory

We have done it!
A trio of Italian players celebrate the the final whistle after beating England on penalties in the 2020 Euros

Team building! *Roberto Mancini with his charges as they progress through the 2020 European Championship to win the competition*

The first Euro victory! *Italian captain Giacinto Facchetti lifts the trophy won in 1968*

In safe hands! Gianluigi Donnarumma has followed in the footsteps of Italy's great goalkeepers from the past

In Competition! Gianluca Scamacca in action against Switzerland's Manuel Akanji in Italy's final game in the round of 16 in the finals of Euro 2024

The Blueprint! The Allianz stadium – the home of Juventus since 2011

consecutive match, Italy found themselves a goal down, but came back to win. A superb strike on the edge of the penalty area from Aleksandr Karapetyan in the 11th minute sent the home fans into raptures and the lead lasted until just before the half-hour mark, when Andrea Belotti converted after a cross from Emerson Palmieri.

There were no further goals before the break, but Armenia's task was made even harder when their goalscorer was dismissed after being shown a second yellow. However, it took until the last 15 minutes for Italy to turn the man advantage into goals. The first came via a header from Lorenzo Pellegrini, then a shot from Belotti hit the unfortunate Aram Ayrapetyan in goal before crossing the line to make the final score 3-1 in favour of Italy.

Three days later and Italy played Finland, who were in second place and thus posing the biggest threat to top-place qualification. Finland started the game in a zealous fashion, pressing the Italians, causing them to make mistakes in defence. However, the best chance fell to Italy when Stefano Sensi's volley was acrobatically saved by Lukas Hradecky.

Italy started to stamp their own authority on proceedings with Sensi once more coming close, Francesco Acerbi having an attempt which was deflected for a corner. Hradecky was again called into action to deny Federico Chiesa from a tight angle, saving with his legs. The first half ended goalless, but it was nearly 1-0 to the home nation just after the break when a Teemu

Pukki shot skewed just wide. Finland were left to rue this chance when Italy took the lead on the hour mark.

A pinpoint cross from Chiesa was met by the head of Immobile, who then powerfully directed the ball past Hradecky to give his nation the lead. The game was then decided by two penalties. Firstly, for Finland after Pukki raced into the penalty area only to be brought down by a challenge from Sensi. This was a double whammy for Sensi, who had lost possession just seconds before. Pukki converted and parity was restored, until Italy were awarded a spot kick themselves in the 79th minute. This time the penalty was converted by Jorginho but wasmired in controversy after a Nicolò Barella shot hit the arm of Sauli Väisänen at point-blank range.

Roberto Mancini was in a reflective mood when he was questioned after the match, which Italy held on to win 2-1: 'We suffered a little, but we caused it ourselves by losing the ball where we shouldn't lose it.' Mancini was also quick to look at the positives, 'On the other hand, there were lots of things that I liked. It's very positive that we dominate games away from home. Our nature is always to attack, and I've seen that again tonight, giving very little of the ball to our opponents.'

Despite the defeat, Finland still remained on course for their first ever major tournament appearance and had pushed Italy all the way.

The seventh and eighth straight victories came in October with a win in Rome against Greece and away in

Liechtenstein, and it was the former result that secured qualification for Italy with three games to play.

There was an unfamiliar look to the group leaders as they took to the pitch in Rome on 12 October. Instead of the traditional Azzurri blue shirts, Italy were in green. It made no difference to the winning streak as they triumphed 2-0. There were no goals in the first half with the host nation having 72 per cent possession of the ball but strangely having no shots on target to show for it.

Greece continued to play a tight tactical game plan but found themselves a goal down just after the hour mark. Lorenzo Insigne's shot was blocked by the arm of Greece defender, Andreas Bouchalakis. The resulting penalty was put away by Jorginho. The lead was doubled on 78 minutes when Federico Bernardeschi scored with a neat shot into the bottom corner from just outside the Greek penalty area.

The team in green celebrated at the final whistle knowing that top spot in the group was now assured and they had just won their eighth consecutive match in all competitions (as well as the friendly win over the USA). Interestingly, this run was now just one short of the record that had been set by Vittorio Pozzo's Italy in the latter part of the 1930s and it was equalled just three days later with a convincing 5-0 win in Liechtenstein.

The first of the five goals was scored in only the second minute of the match when Federico Bernardeschi netted. Surprisingly, Italy did not score again until the final 20 minutes. Headers from Andrea Belotti and

Alessio Romagnoli extended the lead before Stephan El Shaarawy made it four, then Belotti bagged his second in stoppage time with another header.

Inevitably, media questions centred around equalling the record set by Pozzo, and Mancini was still looking forward and not necessarily back in time. 'Am I interested in equalling Pozzo's record? I would be interested in winning two World Cups and an Olympic Games like he did, but a European Championship would do just fine.'

The perfect ten was completed the following month with the final two games of the campaign. Firstly, Italy travelled to Bosnia and Herzegovina on 15 November 2019. There was not much to play for (apart from breaking the record) and the match started casually, until the 21st minute when Francesco Acerbi scored an impressive individual goal. A second on 37 minutes scored by Insigne settled the Italians down before a spectacular strike from Belotti on 52 minutes signalled the end of the scoring, and the start of a brand-new era, with a record ten consecutive wins confirmed.

This was stretched to 11 in spectacular style in Italy's final match of the qualifying campaign against Armenia in Palermo on 18 November 2019, and this is how Susy Campanale from *Football Italia* reported on this historic match:

'Italy broke numerous records with a 9-1 annihilation of Armenia, completing their perfect Euro 2020 qualifying record in Palermo.

The Azzurri concluded their Euro 2020 qualifying campaign, already sure of their status as top seeds, and were seeking another historic victory. It was their 11th in a row, the tenth in one calendar year (both new records) and maintains their perfect tally in Group J.'

Campanale then noted the changes made:

'Roberto Mancini rotated the squad after Friday's 3-0 win away to Bosnia-Herzegovina, bringing in the likes of Alessio Romagnoli, Nicolò Zaniolo, Ciro Immobile and Federico Chiesa. Armenia had Rumyan Hovsepyan suspended, Henrikh Mkhitaryan injured and new coach Abraham Khashmanyan debuted with a 1-0 home defeat to Greece. Armenia's only previous game on Italian soil was a 2-2 draw in October 2013, losing both home fixtures.'

It took eight minutes for Italy to take the lead when Ciro Immobile headed home before turning provider just one minute later. The Lazio striker ran forward with the ball before finding Zaniolo, whose shot went in between the legs of the Armenian goalkeeper, Arma Airapetyan. It was almost 2-1 when a sloppy back-pass from Leonardo Bonucci was intercepted by Aleksandr Karapetyan, who then saw his attempted lob bounce off the bar much to the relief of the Italian team, and none more so than the normally reliable Bonucci.

This served as a warning to the Azzurri and the momentary lapse of reason was addressed with another quick Italian outburst with Bonucci making amends when he sent Barella through, who was able to dink the ball over the keeper. Moments later and it was Zaniolo's turn to assist Immobile, who then proceeded to round the goalkeeper to make it 4-0 after just 33 minutes.

There were no further goals in the first period but it was 5-0 in the 64th minute of the match when Zaniolo scored his second goal. The lead was stretched further in the 72nd minute when Romagnoli scored from a rebound. Italy were awarded a penalty just monents later which was duly converted by Jorginho before substitute Riccardo Orsolini headed home from a cross from Chiesa.

The deficit was reduced to just seven when Edgar Babayan's long-range shot found the back of the Italian net, but the winning margin of eight was confirmed with the final goal of the game when Chiesa headed home from Orsolini's cross.

It had been a momentous campaign for Mancini and his Italian players, with them scoring 37 goals in ten matches, conceding just four. Amazingly, 36 of the goals were shared by 19 players, making it a true team collaboration with one own goal helping proceedings. The leading scorer was Andrea Belotti, who contributed four goals.

UEFA Euro 2020 Qualifying Group J – Final Table

Pos	Team	Pld	W	D	L	GF	GA	GD	Pts
1	Italy	10	10	0	0	37	4	33	30
2	Finland	10	6	0	4	16	10	6	18
3	Greece	10	4	2	4	12	14	-2	14
4	Bosnia and H'a	10	4	1	5	20	17	3	13
5	Armenia	10	3	1	6	14	25	-11	10
6	Liechtenstein	10	0	2	8	2	31	-29	2

Whilst Italy were celebrating perfect qualification and equalling record winning margins, the world was getting news about a coronavirus that was reported to have had its origins in the Huanan seafood wholesale market in Wuhan, central China. Very soon the market became widely known as the epicentre of a virus that, over the coming months, would have a major impact on lives throughout the world. What had likely started in bats soon transmitted to humans in the surrounding areas, then spread to other parts of China and ultimately from country to country. The virus soon became well known as Covid-19, with the strain called SARS-CoV-2. The virus transmitted itself from person to person via droplets from the nose and mouth caused by coughing and sneezing. It soon became apparent that touching contaminated surfaces and skin were also attributable factors.

The first cases in Italy were confirmed in the early part of 2020, after two Chinese tourists tested positive in Rome. A third case soon followed and involved an Italian man repatriated to his native country. What made this even more interesting was that he had come from Wuhan. Over the next few weeks, cases were confirmed in various places. Inevitably, the first deaths were reported, on 22 February. By the beginning of March, there had been cases confirmed in all regions of Italy.

Italy had been one of the first European countries to suffer the pandemic's full impact, and one of the first to respond to it. Initially they had suspended all flights to and from China and this was eventually followed by full lockdowns that were nationwide and not just regional. On 21 March, the Italian government closed all non-essential business and industries save for supermarkets and pharmacies.

The world was slowly but surely closing its borders as the World Health Organisation (WHO) desperately worked around the clock in order to come up with the best solutions to contain and better understand the virus. This would soon impact day to day life, with people told to stay at home, with businesses closing their doors.

Inevitably, sport would also have to play its part. As a consequence, the Euros of 2020 were postponed until the summer of 2021, but would still be known by their original tournament name and have the same hosts. Alongside this, changes were made by UEFA that allowed for two extra substitutes and the introduction of a Video Assistant Referee (VAR).

Italy were ranked at number two for the tournament behind Belgium. They were placed into Group A alongside Wales, Switzerland and Turkey. The first match of the finals was played at the Stadio Olimpico in Rome on 11 June 2021 and saw Italy take on Turkey in front of just under 13,000 fans, with crowds restricted due to the pandemic. Despite the low crowds, the tournament opened in spectacular fashion with a firework display and a beautiful rendition of 'Nessun Dorma' from Andrea Bocelli.

Italy dominated the match from kick-off but could not find the net in the first half. The closest they came was from a Giorgio Chiellini header from a corner which was well saved by Ugurcan Cakir in the Turkish goal. The deadlock was broken eight minutes into the second half when Turkey's centre-half, Merih Demiral, turned the ball into his own net and the lead was doubled when Ciro Immobile pounced on a loose ball after Leonardo Spinazzola's shot was initially blocked by Cakir. Immobile was in the thick of things for the third and final goal when he teed up Insigne, who duly put the ball into the Turkish net with a fine finish. Italy were up and running as they ran out 3-0 winners.

Rome was once again the setting for Italy's second match of the group five days later, when they entertained Switzerland, and produced the same outcome. Just like they had done against Turkey, Italy dominated in the early stages of the match, Chiellini once more coming the closest. This time he did have the ball in the net, but the goal was disallowed for a handball in the build-up after a VAR check. Moments later, the Italian players were celebrating after Manuel Locatelli scored from close range following a determined run and cross from Domenico Beradi.

Locatelli was back on the scoresheet in the 52nd minute. His second goal came from the edge of the penalty area, as he fired a sweet left-foot shot past Yann Sommer in the Swiss goal. The third and final goal was scored in similar circumstances when Immobile's screamer from outside the penalty area beat Sommer at his far post.

Whilst Mancini was quick to admit it had been a hard-fought match, he was full of praise for the attitude shown by his team, 'We went into the game thinking we wanted to win it at all costs. It was a very tough match. We could have scored a second goal a bit earlier. We suffered when we had to suffer but in the end it's a well-deserved victory. It was the second game in five days and the boys have worked a lot. We could have sealed it earlier, but we stayed patient.' Mancini also highlighted the contribution made by Manuel Locatelli, 'Two goals for a midfielder are not easy at all and not a given. Manuel played a great match. His action in the first goal was great.'

The third and final group match was against Wales and once more the venue was the Stadio Olympico in Rome. Italy had already qualified in top spot after the consecutive 3-0 victories and Mancini wisely made changes to the personnel. The confidence emanating from the Italians was once more on show as they dominated possession and chances and the Welsh resolve was broken in the 39th minute when Matteo Pessina netted to give

Italy a half-time lead. It could have been stretched further when a free kick taken by Federico Bernardeschi hit the woodwork. The closest that Wales came to scoring a goal and snatching a draw was in the latter stages when Gareth Bale volleyed over.

Italy had made a perfect start to the competition with three wins, maximum points and not conceding, whilst scoring seven themselves.

Italy's reward was a round of 16 clash with Austria at Wembley Stadium in London on 26 June. The match turned out to be a forerunner for what was to come for the Azzurri in future rounds.

The match (in regulation time) finished goalless. Italy had the best chances in the opening period and could have taken the lead just after the half-hour mark when a powerful shot from Ciro Immobile hit the upright. Austria had the best chance in the second half and had the ball in the net in the 65th minute through their talisman, Marko Arnautović. However, VAR ruled that there had been an offside in the build-up. Italy looked stronger going into extra time and Chiesa opening the scoring in the first five minutes, when he was able to control a cross from Leonardo Spinazzola and put the ball into the Austrian net from a tight angle. Then ten minutes later, Pessina found himself in similar space to fire in the second before Saša Kalajdžić reduced Italy's lead with a glancing header in the last minute of the first period of extra time, but Italy successfully negotiated this potential banana-skin tie, and now it was time for far more robust tests.

Italy's fifth game of the tournament saw them travel to the Allianz Arena in Munich to take on the number-one ranked team in the quarter-finals, Belgium. It was a game that didn't disappoint either, with all three goals scored in a frantic first half. Italy had a goal disallowed early on for offside after Bonucci had bundled the ball home and Gianluigi Donnarumma had to be at his best to keep Belgium out, making important saves. The opening goal came after 31 minutes and it was first blood to Italy, when Marco Verratti found Nicolò Barella, who fired the ball into their opponents' goal. It was 2-0 just before the break, seemingly putting Italy firmly in the driving seat. Lorenzo Insigne picked up the ball in the middle of the park before cutting in and sending a beautifully curling shot into the net. Then just before the half-time whistle was blown, Belgium found a way back into the match when they were awarded a penalty which was converted by Romelu Lukaku. This set up an intriguing second period, but surprisingly there were no further goals, with Italy winning 2-1.

It was back to Wembley Stadium for the semi-final showdown against Spain which was played on 6 July in front of more than 50,000 fans, as permitted crowd numbers were increased in the latter stages of the tournament. The game was a fascinating contest from the start and Italy were unlucky not to take the lead in the first five minutes when a precise chip from Nicolò Barella hit the post, and Spain breathed a huge sigh of relief, which was doubled with the offside flag being raised in any case. The next couple of chances fell to Spain with Mikel Oyarzabal and Ferran Torres in the thick of the action. Spain continued to have the better of the opportunities, but the final chance of the first half fell to Italy when Emerson's shot went narrowly over the bar from a tight angle.

There was no let-up in the second period with both teams having chances before Italy took the lead on the hour mark, Chiesa bending a fine effort into the far corner of the net to send the Italian fans wild. Now it was down to Spain to force the issue, but the Italy players were standing firm, especially with Chiellini in inspired form. But with just ten minutes remaining, Spain were back in the contest with substitute Álvaro Morata scoring. Now the impetus was with Spain, but they could not make the breakthrough as the game went into extra time, and no further goals meant it would be decided on penalties.

The first two spot kicks from both teams were missed before Italy scored their next four, with Jorginho netting the all-important and decisive last one after Morata had failed to convert.

Italy were in their third final of the 21st century, having lost their previous two. This time they were taking on England at Wembley Stadium on Sunday, 11 July 2021. The increase in attendances continued with nearly 68,000 inside Wembley.

The deadlock was broken in the first couple of minutes, and it looked very ominous for Italy as the home nation took the lead. A pass from England's Harry

Kane was perfectly met on the left by Luke Shaw, who smashed the ball past Donnarumma. The first period largely belonged to England without them making any significant chances to double the lead. However, it was Italy who finished it the stronger, and it was no surprise when parity was restored in the 67th minute when Leonardo Bonucci bundled the ball home from close range. Now there looked like there would be only one winner but no further goals were scored in the remaining minutes, plus extra time, so the match ended all square at 1-1.

In the penalty shoot-out, the first two spot-kicks were converted, via Italy's Domenico Berardi and England's Kane. It was advantage England after the next round with Andrea Belotti missing his kick and Harry Maguire converting his. However, two misses by England (by Marcus Rashford and Jadon Sancho) and two conversions by Italy (Leonardo Bonucci and Federico Bernardeschi) meant that if Jorginho scored Italy's fifth penalty then it would be all over for the English. He had scored the decisive penalty in the semi-final but could not repeat this feat, so England were given a lifeline, until a third consecutive penalty miss, this time by Bukayo Saka, meant Italy were European Champions for the first time since 1968, winning 3-2 on penalties.

Roberto Mancini had successfully overseen a golden period in Italy's rich history, when records had been broken and medals won for the first time since 2006. 'It was impossible even to just consider this at one stage, but the guys were just amazing. I have no words for them, this is a wonderful group. This was a difficult game made a lot harder after their early goal. Apart from that early spell, we dominated the match.' Mancini was in a magnanimous mood as he continued with his observations about how the game was decided: 'You have to have a little luck on penalties. I feel a little sorry for England, because they also had a great tournament. The team has grown a lot and I think we can improve further. We are very happy for all Italians. I have no words for these guys!'

There was no time for Mancini and his team to dwell on the victory or indeed rest on their laurels. The pandemic had severely impacted sporting schedules and it was time to move on to qualifying for the next World Cup – or rather go back to it. Italy's qualification quest had started a few months before the Euros in the summer of 2021. They had played three games already and been victorious in all of them, and were sitting top of their group, with their sights set on qualifying for Qatar 2022.

Italy had missed out on the previous World Cup in Russia, and had only failed to qualify for a World Cup once before, and that had been as far back as 1958. The thought of not making it to consecutive World Cups was something that not even the most pessimistic could comprehend. After all, Mancini had cited making Italians happy as one of his aims.

As the sun set on a wonderful summer of football for his nation, surely this was not going to change now?

FIFA World Cup Campaign: 2022

Host nation for the finals: Qatar
Qualifying group: UEFA Group C
Opponents: Switzerland, Northern Ireland,
Bulgaria, Lithuania
Manager: Roberto Mancini

ITALY HAD played three qualifying games before signing off to participate in the delayed 2020 Euros, and the impact of Covid-19 had meant those first three games were played behind closed doors.

The first of these took place at Stadio Ennio Tardini in Parma on 25 March with the hosts welcoming Northern Ireland. A commanding first-half display saw Italy take a 2-0 lead into the break with no further goals scored by either nation in the second period.

Ciro Immobile was in fine form, finding himself close to scoring in the opening exchanges from a volley that he didn't connect with properly. However, the lead that Italy sought was confirmed in the 14th minute of the match, Domenico Berardi scoring after being able to cut inside Stuart Dallas before placing his shot past the Irish goalkeeper from a tight angle. It was Berardi who, more than any other Italian player, started to take control of proceedings, creating chances for both Immobile and Emerson Palmieri which were not converted. The lead was then doubled in the 39th minute after Italy had broken up a rare Northern Ireland attack which allowed Immobile the space to fire into the net.

The second period of the match was a much closer affair with the visitors carving out a couple of chances to get back into the match, but the Italian defence stood firm to begin qualification with a deserved 2-0 victory.

Italy recorded a second successive 2-0 win just three days later at the Vasil Levski National Stadium in Sofia, against Bulgaria.

Surprisingly, Italy had never won a competitive match in Bulgaria and nearly found themselves a goal down early on when Andrey Galabinov fired a shot, but it was straight at Gianluigi Donnarumma. Italy came back into the contest and Chiesa was causing issues before a timely intervention prevented him from doing any real damage and the Juventus winger failed to control a Lorenzo Insigne pass shortly after. There were also chances for Insigne and Belotti before the Italians finally made the breakthrough when they were awarded a penalty just before half-time for a foul on Belotti as he ran on to a slide-rule pass from Insigne. The Torino striker duly stepped up to convert the spot kick and send his country into a 1-0 half-time lead.

There were further penalty appeals turned down for both teams in the second period. It was nearly 2-0 to the away side in the 72nd minute, a lob from Belotti hitting the base of the upright before he fired over the rebound. Italy's second goal came in the 83rd minute when substitute Manuel Locatelli curled a superb right-foot finish into the far corner, for his first goal for his country. Italy were now in total control and had chances to extend their lead when Immobile was sent clear from Leonardo Bonucci but hit his shot straight at the on-rushing Bulgarian shot-stopper before seeing another chance saved shortly after.

Italy's final game before the Euros took place on 31 March with yet another 2-0 victory (to make it three consecutive wins by the same margin), against Lithuania in Vilnius. Roberto Mancini made ten changes to the side which had beaten Bulgaria just a few days before and that changed the pattern of play, as Italy struggled to break down their opponents.

Italy had to wait until after the break to finally quash the Lithuanian resistance when substitute Stefano Sensi fired in the opening goal on 48 minutes. This did not signal an expected goal rush though and Italy had to wait until stoppage time to double their lead, when Immobile converted a penalty. The win put the Azzurri top of the group with three wins and nine points amassed in the process, and no goals conceded.

Italy were now 25 matches unbeaten under Mancini, a joint record shared with Marcelo Lippi, and Mancini took questions from RAI Sport: 'The pitch was difficult, and it wasn't even wet. We still had many chances to score.' Mancini was in a confident mood as he continued, 'The glass is half full. Switzerland only won 1-0 at home against Lithuania three days ago. These matches are always tough. You cannot be brilliant all the time, but the important thing was to win.'

Italy's next match in the qualifying group came just a few weeks after winning the Euros. Their opponents were Bulgaria, and it was played at Stadio Artemio Franchi in Florence. This was a homecoming match after the glories in the summer and was their first qualifying match played in front of fans with a crowd of just over 14,000 in attendance. The effects of the pandemic were still being felt.

The winning feeling was still being felt as well, as Italy went ahead after 16 minutes when Federico Chiesa scored with a fine finish after cleverly linking up with Immobile. Italy were sensing blood. However, Bulgaria equalised against the run of play with five minutes of the first half to go, when Atanas Iliev restored parity. This was the first goal Italy had conceded in the qualifying group and Bulgaria's first real chance of the match.

The second period was dominated by the Italians as they sought a way to make it four consecutive wins. Despite the possession, their only real chance fell to Immobile from a tight angle and it was cleared off the line. The match finished all square at 1-1 but despite the draw, Italy still led the way in the group with ten points, although Switzerland had games in hand. Leonardo Bonucci was in a philosophical mood after the match as he explained to RAI Sport, 'We had opportunities to win, we were too hasty and a bit wasteful in possession. We wanted to celebrate the new start with a victory in front of our fans.'

Roberto Mancini was in a similar frame of mind: 'We came here, the first game after the European Championship, and you want to win it, but I can't say anything bad about the performance, just to be more clinical in front of goal.'

The next match was against Switzerland and was played at the St Jakob-Park in Basel. It ended without a goal being scored and whilst that may have suited Italy more than the home team, in most Italian quarters it was believed it should have been three points as opposed to just one, and it would prove crucial in the final standings.

In the 51st minute of the match, Domenico Berardi was upended in the penalty area by Ricardo Rodríguez. The spot kick was taken by Jorginho who failed to capitalise on this great opportunity, as his right-footed shot was saved by Yann Sommer in the bottom-right corner of the Swiss goal.

Italy were back to winning ways just three days later when they entertained Lithuania at the Mapei Stadium – Città del Tricolore in Reggio Emilia on 8 September, as they were four goals to the good in a blistering opening half-hour of the match.

The Italian press had called for a freshening up of the attack after the team had scored just one goal in the previous two games and Mancini responded with eight changes to a somewhat injury-depleted side. Moise Kean and Giacomo Raspadori made significant impacts.

Firstly, it was Kean who justified his selection when he pounced on a sloppy back-pass to net from close range after just 11 minutes. The lead was doubled three minutes later when a shot from Raspadori was deflected into the back of the net by the unfortunate Edgaras Utkus. It was 3-0 ten minutes later and this time there was no deflection when Raspadori netted with a simple close-range effort before Kean was back on the scoring trail with his second and Italy's fourth in the 29th minute, with a cushioned volley into the top corner. There was only one more goal, in the second half, with Giovanni Di Lorenzo wrapping up proceedings in the 54th minute.

Italy's delight at winning the match 5-0 was further compounded with news that Switzerland and Northern Ireland had played out a goalless draw on the same evening in Belfast, which meant that Italy topped the group with 14 points, six ahead of second-placed Switzerland. Lithuania remained bottom with zero points. The next two rounds of matches were played with Italy sitting them out, and Switzerland taking up their games in hand. The response from the Swiss was perfect with a 2-0 home win against Northern Ireland and a 4-0 victory in Lithuania.

It was all to play for when Italy hosted Switzerland at the Stadio Olimpico in Rome on 12 November. It was certainly a night of high drama for those on the pitch and those in the stadium. The Swiss made the better start and they were rewarded with the game's first goal in the 11th minute. An Italian counter-attack was broken down which allowed Noah Okafor the time to carry the ball forward with speed and tenacity before calmly finding the on-rushing Silvan Widmer, who picked his spot before firing into the net with power and precision.

It was the Swiss who continued to ask the questions, but Italy were back in the match in the 36th minute when Giovanni Di Lorenzo was able to head the ball home from a free kick. The score remained 1-1 and the match was testament to the attitude of both sets of players who were fully aware of what was at stake for both nations. In the dying moments, Italy were awarded a penalty after VAR was used to confirm that Ulisses Garcia had shoved Domenico Berardi. Up stepped Jorginho. His penalty in the game in Switzerland had been well saved, but this time his shot blazed over the bar.

The draw meant that both nations had it all to play for in their final qualifying matches which would be played on 15 November 2021. They were level on 15 points but Italy still led the group with a better goal difference, by two. Italy travelled away to Northern Ireland, while Switzerland hosted Bulgaria.

Northern Ireland's tactics were clear from the very start as they set out to frustrate Italy, who started the match without a recognised striker in the absence of Immobile. Northern Ireland's home campaign had not been one of excitement and fever in terms of goal-mouth activity. They had not conceded any goals and had recorded only one themselves when they had beaten Lithuania just days before.

Italy created few chances in the opening period and their best came when an effort from Di Lorenzo from a tight angle was well saved by Bailey Peacock-Farrell. Opportunities were still at a premium for both nations in the second period of the match, with George Saville coming close for the Irish and Federico Chiesa drilling a shot just wide at the other end. Despite bringing on more forward options, Mancini's side simply could not break down their hosts and the match ended without any goals scored.

This had not been the case in Lucerne though, as Switzerland romped home to top the group with a comprehensive 4-0 victory against Bulgaria. Italy would now have to qualify via the play-offs.

2022 FIFA World Cup Qualification – UEFA Group C Final Table

Pos	Team	Pld	W	D	L	GF	GA	GD	Pts
1	Switzerland	8	5	3	0	15	2	13	18
2	Italy	8	4	4	0	13	2	11	16
3	Northern Ireland	8	2	3	3	6	7	-1	9
4	Bulgaria	8	2	2	4	6	14	-8	8
5	Lithuania	8	1	0	7	4	19	-15	3

There were changes made to the play-off stages for the 2022 World Cup. They would not be contested in two-legged finals as had previously been the case; instead 12 teams were grouped into three different 'paths' which featured two single-leg semi-finals and one single-leg final. The winners of each play-off path final qualified for the finals in Qatar.

The semi-finals were hosted by the six best-ranked runners-up of the qualifying group stage, while the hosts of each final was determined by a draw.

Italy were drawn against North Macedonia in Path C's semi-final with the winners set to play the winners of the Portugal v Turkey match in the final. Both semi-final matches took place on 24 March 2022, with Italy playing at the Stadio Renzo Barbera in Palermo.

The smart money was on Italian qualification for a final encounter against Portugal just five days later. A routine victory for the Azzurri was widely expected, especially on home soil. However, events would be anything but routine.

It seemed very much like it would go to plan in the opening exchanges with Mancini's side looking the brighter of the teams but as the match progressed, North Macedonia's defensive game plan came to the fore, with each of their players giving everything for the cause. Visar Musliu caught the full force of a Domenico Berardi volley in the groin. Berardi was Italy's most effective player and came close to putting them in front on two separate occasions. Firstly, the Sassuolo forward could not control the ball effectively when the North Macedonian keeper, Stole Dimitrievski, had left his goal unguarded. The second chance saw the striker fire an effort over the bar with just the keeper to beat.

It looked increasingly like the match would be going into extra time, but against the run of play and in the dying moments, North Macedonia scored what turned out to be the winning goal. Aleksandar Trajkovski had once played for Palermo and had scored 16 times for the Italian club. However, not one of them was as important as the goal he scored for his home nation after chesting the ball away from two Italian players before setting off towards Gianluigi Donnarumma's goal and putting North Macedonia into the lead with a well-placed shot from just outside the penalty area.

The final whistle was blown soon after and Italy had failed to reach the World Cup finals for a second consecutive campaign, despite being crowned European Champions less than a year previously.

The Italian players and management were honest in their appraisals after the match.

Giorgio Chiellini said, 'It is clear that we are destroyed and crushed, a great void will remain within us. There is a great disappointment. Even today we played a good game, but we couldn't score. From September to today we have made mistakes and we have paid for them.'

Marco Verratti said, 'This group would have had a great chance at the World Cup. We came from the unbeaten record, so it is difficult to accept what happened tonight. We all know that we have given everything. Now surely it is time to ask ourselves some questions.'

Roberto Mancini added, 'It's hard to say something right now – I don't know what to say. Last summer was the most beautiful joy, now comes the greatest disappointment. It is not easy to think of other things. I am very sorry for the boys: I love them much more tonight than in July. I am the coach, I am the first responsible, the boys are not. They have a great future; they are strong players for the future of the national team. We did not deserve this defeat.'

This was as good as it got for North Macedonia, who were knocked out by Portugal in Porto just five days later, 2-0. The finals, played in Qatar in November and December 2022, were won by Argentina, who beat France on penalties in a thrilling match, after the nations shared six goals in 120 minutes. Kylián Mbappé scored all three of France's goals, becoming the second player to score a hat-trick in a final, following Geoff Hurst for England in their 4-2 victory over West Germany at Wembley in 1966.

UEFA European Championship Campaign: 2024

Host nation for the finals: Germany
Qualifying group: UEFA Group C
Opponents: England, Ukraine, North Macedonia, Malta
Manager: Roberto Mancini/Luciano Spalletti

ITALY'S FIRST game of this qualifying campaign brought together the winners and the runners-up of the previous Euros as England were the visitors to the Stadio Diego Armando Maradona in Naples on 23 March 2023 – the first time that the stadium had been used for an Italian home match in a decade. The choice of venue was made with a purpose. It was not the most aesthetically pleasing of stadiums but was one that could be intimidating for the opposition, so the intention was to make England feel as uncomfortable as possible. In the end the decision was one that backfired, leaving the home nation bewildered as England took the game to Italy and in the process, a two-goal lead into the break.

England were a goal to the good as early as the 13th minute when Declan Rice fired in from close range after a shot from Harry Kane was blocked. Kane was looking for his 54th goal for his nation, which would have taken him into the record books as England's leading goalscorer, and was looking very lively. England were awarded a penalty in the 44th minute and it was Kane who buried the chance when he placed the ball past Gianluigi Donnarumma to make history. It was very nearly 3-0 just moments later but England's Jack Grealish was guilty of a dreadful miss. The Italian players breathed a huge sigh of relief when the half-time whistle was blown whilst the fans were in unison in whistling and generally letting the team know of their feelings following first-half events.

Italy were back in the match in the 56th minute after poor work from Harry Maguire, who failed to close down the offensive danger created by Italy as they capitalised on a mistake to allow Mateo Retegui (who was making his debut) to drill a shot past Jordan Pickford from the edge of the penalty area. Despite the fortunate nature of the goal, Italy were not able to break down the English wall as they held firm, despite having Luke Shaw sent off for a second yellow card with ten minutes of the match remaining.

England had won the opening Group C match 2-1 whilst serving the Italians with an ice-cold dish of revenge.

Italy were back on the winning trail just three days later when they travelled to play Malta, this time taking the game to their opponents in the same way as England had done in the previous match. Malta did nothing to help themselves as their formation was very much one of caution. Despite this, Malta almost opened the scoring when Alexander Satariano sent a half-volley towards the Italian goal. However, any celebrations by Malta were cut short when goalkeeper Gianluigi Donnarumma managed to get his fingertips to the ball and push it over the bar.

Italy responded in perfect fashion and took the lead themselves in the 15th minute, when Mateo Retegui was able to shake off his marker to power a header in from a corner. This was his second goal of the competition in only his second appearance for his country. The lead was doubled 12 minutes later when Matteo Pessina scored from close range after a cross from Emerson. It was very nearly three goals to the visitors shortly after, but a Vincenzo Grifo effort was blocked by the Maltese goalkeeper, Henry Bonello.

The pattern of play followed a similar trajectory in the second period of the match with the best chance falling to Gianluca Scamacca, whose overhead kick was saved by Bonello, who once more played his part in keeping the score respectable.

Roberto Mancini was quick to note that although his team won the game quite comfortably, there was room for more improvement, as he told RAI Sport: 'We could've done everything better, that's for sure. When you are 2-0 up, you have the chance to play with less pressure and we should've made more of that.' Mancini continued with his analysis of the match, 'These are games where you have everything to lose, and they tend to be ugly. We did some things well, others less so, both the important thing was to win. We broke the deadlock early and could've scored more, but these matches can be strange.'

The margin of victory was matched by England who comfortably beat Ukraine 2-0 to put Gareth Southgate's team in control of Group C as the early pace-setters.

Italy's third match of the qualifying group took place almost six months after their second one and gave them an ideal opportunity to exact revenge upon North Macedonia, who had knocked them out of the 2022 World Cup qualifiers. The match was played at the Toše Proeski Arena, and before it there would be a changing of the guard in the Italian managerial hot seat.

On 13 August 2023, the Italian Football Federation issued a short announcement that shook the football world:

'The Italian Football Federation announces that it has taken note of the resignation of Roberto Mancini from the position of coach of the Italian national team, received late yesterday evening. Thus concludes a significant page in the history of the Azzurri, which began in May 2018 and concluded with the 2023 Nations League Finals; in between, the victory at Euro 2020, a triumph conquered by a group in which all the individuals have known how to become a team.'

Whilst the federation was quick to thank Mancini for his efforts in which records were broken as well as securing a major trophy, they also pointed to announcing his successor as soon as possible:

> 'Taking into account the important and close commitments for the UEFA Euro 2024 qualifiers (9 and 12 September with North Macedonia and Ukraine), the FIGC will announce the name of the new national coach in the next few days.'

Roberto Mancini used social media platforms to express his gratitude for the five years that he had been in charge of the national team. The now ex-Italy manager said, 'I thank all my players and fans who have accompanied me in these five years. I will always carry the extraordinary victory of the 2020 European Championship in my heart. It has been an honour.'

The need to bring in a new manager was now priority one for the Federation, and on 18 August, Luciano Spalletti was confirmed in the role.

Spalletti's playing career had been in the lower regions of domestic football in Italy and he was still playing semi-professional football in his mid-20s. He retired in 1993 when playing for Empoli before taking up the managerial role there until 1998. By the time he was announced as Italy's manager, he had managed several other Italian clubs. Most notable were Roma (twice), Inter Milan and

Napoli. Spalletti also managed in Russia with Zenit Saint Petersburg as well.

In the match against North Macedonia, Italy had a golden chance to take the lead as early as the third minute when midfielder Nicolò Barella netted, but the celebrations were cut short when his effort was correctly judged to be offside. Despite being second best in terms of possession, the hosts nearly took the lead themselves shortly afterwards. A diving header from Bojan Miovski looked goalbound, but much to the relief of the Italian defence, the ball went wide instead. Sandro Tonali went closer when his low drive hit the post and Italy's dominance continued after Bryan Cristante was denied by goalkeeper Stole Dimitrievski from close range.

Italy should have taken the lead before the first half concluded, but they made amends when Ciro Immobile scored, just moments into the second period. The lead lasted until the 81st minute when North Macedonia's attacking midfielder, Enis Bardhi, levelled the tie and, with no further goals being scored, the match finished all square at 1-1.

It was back to the San Siro in Milan three days later to host Ukraine for Spalletti's first match in charge of the national team on home soil. The deadlock was broken in the 12th minute, and it was delight for the home nation and their new manager. Mattia Zaccagni retrieved the ball on the left-hand side before playing it to Davide Frattesi, who found the net with a sweet shot. The same player scored his second goal just before the half-hour mark when he once more calmly slotted home from close range. The deficit was reduced to one again just four minutes from the break to give Ukraine hope, when Andriy Yarmolenko stabbed the ball home from close range.

Despite exerting considerable pressure in the second half, Ukraine were not able to break the blue wall, with Italy reducing the away nation to half-chances that could not be converted. In fact, the best chance fell to the home nation when a Manuel Locatelli effort struck the crossbar.

Italy won the game 2-1, much to the delight of their new manager, although he expressed caution about how Italy should be killing off opponents more clinically: 'In the final minutes, they [Ukraine] left several players in attack as losing with a larger goal difference wouldn't change much for them. However, we need to be better at scoring the third and fourth goal when we can.'

There were no such worries for Spalletti in the next match a month later, as his players took heed, recording Italy's biggest win of the campaign, against Malta at the Stadio San Nicola in Bari. There was delight for Giacomo Bonaventura in the 23rd minute as he scored his first international goal, when his right-foot curler from the edge of the Maltese penalty area sailed into the top corner. The superb execution was made even more special as the midfielder became the oldest Italy player to score his debut goal for the national team, ten years after making his debut and at the ripe old age of 34. 'Sorry it took so long, I got there eventually,' he told Sky Sports Italia. 'I was lucky, it went well ... these games against a very defensive team are tough to open the scoring.'

The lead was increased on the stroke of half-time to put the home nation in total control. The first goal had been scored courtesy of a right-foot curler and the second from Domenico Berardi was a left-footed effort. The game was put firmly out of reach in the 64th minute when Beradi added to his tally before Frattesi scored the final goal of the night, his low drive from the edge of the penalty area concluding events which left Spalletti waxing lyrical about his team's determined approach to the match and ensuring no banana skin. 'The important thing is the three points, never letting it be in doubt, without taking this test lightly, showing a professional attitude,' Spalletti told RAI Sport. 'You can see these players are eager to get to know each other more and play good football, so we are pretty pleased.'

Italy's next match saw them travel to Wembley Stadium to play England – the scene of their 2021 Euro triumph. It was a match that they simply had to win to stand any chance of finishing top of the group at the expense of their hosts.

It looked like it was going to plan when Italy took the lead against the run of play in the 15th minute, when Gianluca Scamacca netted from a cross from Giovanni Di Lorenzo to send the Italy fans wild as well as the players themselves. However, England were level in the 32nd minute when Jude Bellingham was judged to have been brought down in the penalty area. The penalty was clinically put away by Kane after a lengthy VAR deliberation.

The first half finished all square, but it was England who took the game to the Italians in the second period, scoring two further goals to cement top place in the group and qualification. Firstly, Marcus Rashford fired in a thunderous effort before Kane scored his second and England's third goal to win the match 3-1.

The defeat left Italy on ten points and in a straight battle with Ukraine for the second qualifying spot from the group. There were two games left and Italy's next match was against North Macedonia in Rome on 17 November 2023.

In a match that Italy simply had to win, they broke the deadlock after 17 minutes much to the relief of the Azzurri faithful. Matteo Darmian headed in a corner after being left unmarked. Italy were awarded a penalty with just five minutes of the first half remaining, but Italian nerves were still being tested when Jorginho's attempt was saved. However, the nerves were being waved goodbye when the disappointment of missing the penalty was turned around with two more goals in the dying minutes of the half, thanks to efforts from Federico Chiesa. The first was a curling shot from the edge of the box and the second was via a deflected shot that looped into the top corner.

North Macedonia were back in the match seven minutes after the restart when Jani Atanasov nodded in from close range. Amazingly, the deficit was reduced to just one goal when the same player scored his second following a long-range shot that took a significant deflection. Any chance of North Macedonia inflicting further pain on the Italians was firmly dashed in the final ten minutes, however, when Italy scored two more goals, from Giacomo Raspadori and Stephan El Shaarawy, to win the match 5-2.

That last match took place against Ukraine at the BayArena in Leverkusen, Germany on 20 November. It was played in a neutral country due to the ongoing Russia/Ukraine conflict.

The maths was simple for Italian qualification. If they did not lose the match, it would be them going through at the expense of Ukraine, who would then have to qualify through the play-offs.

Italy came close to opening the scoring in the seventh minute when Chiesa's effort flew narrowly over the bar before Ukraine had a shot from Georgiy Sudakov saved by Donnarumma, then Italy started to dominate the game and came close on two separate occasions in the first period, firstly from a Di Lorenzo header and then a Frattesi shot, which was superbly saved by Trubin in the Ukraine goal.

The second half contained few chances from either team and the closest that any side came was in the 66th minute when Mudryk was denied by Donnarumma. The match ended scoreless, with Italy qualifying in second place in the group.

UEFA Euro 2024 Qualifying Group C
Final Table

Pos	Team	Pld	W	D	L	GF	GA	GD	Pts
1	England	8	6	2	0	22	4	18	20
2	Italy	8	4	2	2	16	9	7	14
3	Ukraine	8	4	2	2	11	8	3	14[a]
4	North Macedonia	8	2	2	4	10	20	-10	8
5	Malta	8	0	0	8	2	20	-18	0

For the finals themselves, Italy were drawn alongside Spain, Croatia and Albania in Group B.

Their first match took place on 15 June at the home of Borussia Dortmund where they played Albania, and the first goal the champions conceded was just 23 seconds in the making, creating history as the fastest goal ever scored in the finals. Italy were awarded a throw-in which was taken by Federico Dimarco. With the pre-match anthems still ringing around the stadium, Dimarco's wayward throw was seized upon by Nedim Bajrami, reacting long before the Italian defence did, and his powerful drive hit the back of the Italian net.

Albania were in dreamland and the Italians were shell-shocked, but this didn't last for long, as Italy showed why they were the defending champions and parity was restored after 11 minutes. A powerful header from an unmarked Alessandro Bastoni found the back of the net following a short corner. Five minutes later and the turnaround was completed when a superb strike from Nicolò Barella sailed past Thomas Strakosha in the Albanian goal.

It had been a frantic opening exchange, but the champions were then able to start controlling the game with measured passing before hitting their opponents hard and fast. Despite dominating the rest of the match, chances were few and far between. Italy's best opportunities to add to their tally came when Gianluca Scamacca was denied by Strakosha, who was then also called into action to brilliantly turn a shot from Nicolò Fagioli on to the post. Italy were almost left to rue these chances when Albanian substitute Rey Manaj saw an effort go just wide, much to the relief of the Italian defence, as they held on to win the opening match, 2-1.

Italy's next game was a mouth-watering clash with Spain that took place at the Arena Aufschalke on 20 June. Matches between Italy and Spain seldom disappoint, and this game was no exception, although it was Spain who dominated from start to finish. The Italian defence had been breached in seconds in the previous match, and Spain also came close in the early exchanges. Nico Williams was a thorn in the Italian side all evening and showed his intentions very early on with some left-wing trickery that resulted in a cross to the head of Pedri, whose effort was tipped over by Gianluigi Donnarumma. Williams should have scored himself with a header in the tenth minute, but sent it wide when he found space in front of goal. Donnarumma was in the thick of things when he blocked an angled effort from Álvaro Morata before following this up to flick over a long-range drive from Fabián Ruiz.

Apart from runs from Federico Dimarco down the left, Italy offered very little offensive play and it was Spain asking all the important questions. This was not lost on Luciano Spalletti, who brought on Bryan Cristante and Andrea Cambiaso at the break. Despite this, it was still the Spaniards running the match as they had done in the first period, and they really should have taken the lead when Pedri fired wide after good play from Marc Cucurella. Such was the dominance from Spain, the question was not if they would score at all but when, and in the 55th minute it was answered. Williams had once more terrorised the Italian left side of defence, before his cross was flicked on by Morata. Donnarumma could only get his fingertips to the header, and the ball rebounded in off the unfortunate Riccardo Calafiori.

The momentum remained with Spain and Donnarumma was soon back in action when he tipped over another effort from the lively Morata, and Spain were unlucky not to extend their lead.

Firstly, Cambiaso cleared off his line and Lamine Yamal curled a shot just wide. Williams came closer when he cut in from the left before unleashing a shot against the Italian crossbar. The one and only real chance for the defending champions came in the dying minutes but Cristante's flick was comfortably gathered by Unai Simón. There was still time for Spain to attempt to increase their lead, with Donnarumma denying Ayoze Pérez on a couple of occasions before the final whistle blew with Spain winning 1-0.

Italy's manager and their man of the match were both in reflective mood afterwards.

Spalletti said: 'There were too many gaps, all over the pitch. We were constantly stretched; we were never able to squeeze the gaps between the various units and they were able to cause us problems. They caused us more problems than the scoreline suggests – let's not beat about the bush.'

Donnarumma commented: 'Honestly, I don't care about my saves – I was hoping for a different result and a different performance. We missed too many easy passes and put in too little quality and, if you miss that much, they punish you.'

The defeat left Italy in second place on three points, with Spain having already qualified from the group stages with their second successive win.

Italy's third and final game in the group took place against Croatia on 24 June in Leipzig. With so much at stake for both countries, the first 20 minutes saw the ball dominated by the Croatians with very little creative output in front of goal. The only exception was a long-range shot from Luka Sučić which was parried over by Donnarumma. Italy had been content to sit back in the opening stages but looked far more of a threat soon after with a couple of half-chances via Mateo Retegui. However, the best chance of the half fell to Alessandro Bastoni, whose powerful header from a cross from Nicolò Barella was saved by Dominik Livaković in the Croatian goal. The first half ended with Italy in the ascendency, but it was 45 minutes that had not produced anything of any real quality. If the match finished as a draw, with Spain beating Albania 1-0, Italy would qualify in second place.

However, the tables were turned in the opening exchanges of the second period when Croatia took the lead. A hopeful shot from Andrej Kramarić struck the arm of Davide Frattesi, who had been a half-time substitute for the Azzurri. Initially the referee (Danny Makkelie) waved play on, much to the dismay of the Croatian players. However, the dismay soon turned to joy when the penalty was given after VAR intervention sent the official to the screen. The penalty was taken by Luka Modric but was brilliantly saved by Donnarumma low to the left. The ball was kept in play and was back with the Croatians, a cross from the left was met by another half-time substitute, Ante Budimir, and his header was brilliantly saved by the Italian shot-stopper, but Modric was on hand to follow up and put the ball into the net, to atone for his penalty miss. The goal put Modric into the record books as the oldest scorer in European Championship history.

The 1-0 lead afforded to Croatia put them in pole position to finish in second place and progress to the knockout rounds at the expense of the current champions. If the score stayed the same, then Italy would have to play the waiting game and see if they qualified as one of the best third-placed nations in the competition.

As expected, it was all Italy in the closing stages of the match and the closest that they came to restoring parity was when Scamacca was just inches from connecting with a cross in the 87th minute. There had been a number of second-half substitutions made by both teams which resulted in eight minutes of stoppage time, and it was in the 98th minute that Croatian hearts were broken when Italy deservedly equalised when Mattia Zaccagni curled home a beautiful shot from the left-hand side that sailed into the back of the net and out of reach of the Croatian keeper. The match ended just seconds later with Italy going through to the knockout stages in second place in the group on four points, leaving Croatia in third place with very slim hopes of being one of the best third-placed teams as they finished on just two points.

Understandably both the Italian manager and the goalscorer were in a positive mood when giving their assessments of the game in the post-match interviews. Spalletti said, 'We passed through the group stage with merit. Now we will have a chance to think about the next match [in the last 16].'

'Immense satisfaction, I'm excited, it's a beautiful evening,' Zaccagni said. 'It was important to draw to qualify in second place. We did well to stay in the game with a great second half. We deserved this draw. The coach did well to create this group– we will try to repay him on the pitch.'

That 'next match' that Spalletti mentioned saw Italy play Switzerland at the Olympiastadion in Berlin on Saturday, 29 June in the round of 16 – the first knockout round of the tournament, at the scene of one of Italy's greatest ever matches in 2006. The first point of interest regarding the match came in the form of Spalletti making six changes from the team that had started against Croatia. The most notable change was bringing in Scamacca and dropping Jorginho.

It was the Swiss team that posed the questions in the early stages of the game, and they troubled the Italian defence in the first few seconds when Breet Embolo got the better of the offside trap after being fed through by Fabian Schär. The ball deflected off Bryan Christante and had Donnarumma scrambling. Switzerland continued to hold court as they looked confident and aggressive on the ball with Granit Xhaka superbly dictating the play for his nation.

Embolo once more breached the offside trap, but his lethargic effort was easily saved by Donnarumma. Switzerland's domination continued at a pace that saw them having well over 60 per cent of the possession in the opening half-hour of the match, with Italy retreating at an alarming rate and going deeper and deeper. It was only a matter of time before the Swiss would turn their superiority into a lead and the goal came on 37 minutes. Rubén Vargas's pass into the box found the onrushing Remo Freuler, who was able to control the ball before firing his shot past Donnarumma. It was no more than the Swiss deserved, and the lead could have been doubled soon after when a free kick from Rieder was pushed on to the post by Donnarumma and out for a corner.

If it had been a boxing contest as opposed to a football match, it may have been stopped at half-time by the referee as the Swiss had put together over 30 shots with ten of them on target. Italy had attempted just five shots with only one on target. Spalletti's response was instant as Stephan El Shaarawy was replaced by the group-stage hero, Zaccagni. However, a more instant impact was made by the second goal scored by the Swiss at the start of the second period. Michel Aebischer looked to have his work cut out when he was surrounded by three Italian players, but before the players in blue had time to react, the ball was played to Vargas, who got the better of his markers before finding the top corner of the net. The defending champions were simply stunned by this and offered no real challenge for the rest of the match, apart from an effort from Scamacca which hit the post. The final whistle was blown, and Italy were sent crashing out of the finals with a 2-0 defeat that actually flattered them, such was the dominance of Switzerland, who simply outclassed their opponents from the first whistle to the last.

Spalletti's decision to ring the changes had backfired. Whilst the Swiss players played as a team with a great understanding, Italy did not. Whilst the Swiss played as a team with a great understanding, Italy did not and the energy to do so was clearly lacking.

Spalletti was once more in a philosophical mood after the match. 'The results have said that we need to change things. That's been the footballing verdict, and I'll be forced to do so.'

The Italian manager was then asked the inevitable question about whether he would remain in his position after the dust had settled on a campaign that never really got started for the Azzurri. 'That question is only natural, don't feel guilty about asking me that question, but it comes to the crux of that matter. It doesn't change anything for me; I have responsibility for what happened, I picked the players, and this is part of a process where I have to get to know players.

'I'm not happy with the performance. I wasn't happy with the performance against Spain. I am partially happy with the other two matches we played but we were under par tonight and against Spain. On the other occasion I thought it was down to me having barked at them at training. This time I rested them and changed the team, whereas in the previous game I blamed it on myself regardless of general team selection.'

The only player who could well and truly hold his head up high was Donnarumma. The Paris Saint Germain goalkeeper had been player of the tournament three years earlier when Italy were crowned European Champions and, in Germany, he was once more Italy's most prized asset. The shot-stopper had made crucial saves in all of Italy's group matches.

The winners of the competition were Spain, who defeated England 2-1 in the final.

Why the Apocalypse
Bore a Blue Hue …

THE SKIES may have been turning blue in Berlin on 9 July 2006 as Fabio Cannavaro lifted the World Cup trophy for his beloved nation on the international stage, but darker clouds had been forming over Italy and its domestic game in the weeks leading up to the final, especially thickening in Turin, the home of Italian champions, Juventus.

The club supplied eight of the players who had fought for world supremacy in Germany that day – five in the Italy team and three in the French – but everything in the garden was not rosy. What had started as an initial investigation into potential doping at Juventus metamorphosed into something that was much larger and more widespread, with far greater implications for Italian football than just in Turin.

Known as *Calciopoli*, the scandal was first reported in May 2006. An investigation into doping had serendipitously uncovered a number of telephone tappings which highlighted relations between the club's executives and referee organisations during the previous two seasons (2004/05 and 2005/06). Now the real story involved accusations that Juventus were being given 'favourable' officials for their matches – and this was not confined to the Italian champions. Other clubs began to be implicated. These included Fiorentina, Lazio, AC Milan and Reggina.

In the same month as Italy were crowned World Champions, their domestic champions were stripped of the 2005/06 title. Not only that, but Juventus were demoted to Serie B with a significant points deduction to follow. Unsurprisingly, the club experienced a mass exodus of key players who sought to continue playing at the highest level, although it is important to note that the likes of Gianluigi Buffon, Alessandro Del Piero, Giorgio Chiellini, Pavel Nedved and David Trezeguet, all international stars and among the best of their era, decided to stay. The financial implications were also a massive contribution to the club's downfall.

The biggest example was certainly made of the biggest club, but relegation was also given to Fiorentina and Lazio (although this was later overturned on appeal) and all five clubs received points deductions for the following season. The sanctions for each club were as follows:

Juventus
Original punishment: Relegated to Serie B, -30 points
Final punishment: Relegated to Serie B, -9 points
Other punishments: Stripped of 2004/05 Serie A title, downgraded to bottom of 2005/06 table.

AC Milan

Original punishment: -15 points

Final punishment: -8 points

Other punishments: Deducted 30 points from 2005/06 season.

Fiorentina

Original punishment: Relegated to Serie B, -12 points

Final punishment: -15 points in Serie A

Other punishments: Ejected from 2006/07 Champions League.

Lazio

Original punishment: Relegated to Serie B, -7 points

Final punishment: -3 points in Serie A

Other punishments: Ejected from 2006/07 UEFA Cup.

Reggina

Original punishment: -15 points

Final punishment: -11 points

Other punishments: €100,000 fine.

As a result of the multi-faceted punishments given out to those clubs, it was not a total surprise that many prison sentences were handed out to people caught up in the affair.

There can be no doubt that the *Calciopoli* scandal of 2006 not only altered the course of Juventus's immediate future but also Italian football in general. The juxtaposition could not have been more expansive, with the success on the world stage at the same time. History has decreed that the Italian national team prosper when the domestic clubs perform well. The scandal had a seismic impact on that theory. That's why Italy's win in Berlin was not only unexpected but remarkable given that the scandal came to light as the national team started to prepare for the finals. There were calls for Italy not to participate in the tournament and players were asked to assist in the investigation. Preparations for the finals were dominated by the scandal and not the progress of any of the players in the camp. Indeed, fans turned up to voice their displeasure pertaining to the scene that was unfolding almost on an hourly basis at times.

Match fixing in all its forms and doping had been a staple diet of Italian football for time immemorial, but nothing had been seen on the scale of *Calciopoli* before. By the end of the World Cup, Italians were unable to remove the images of Cannavaro lifting the World Cup and phone tapping from their minds. A bittersweet feeling if ever there was one in team sport.

The question on everyone's lips centred around the long-term effects this would have on Italian football both domestically and internationally. Initially a conversation about the need for transparency and true accountability was required, which would serve as a major starting point, in simple black and white. Over the coming weeks, months and years, layers of grey nuance would be added.

Calciopoli hit Italian football hard and made a mockery of Serie A's standing in not only European football, but also the world itself. The 1980s and the 1990s had been the golden age of Serie A, especially after the World Cup which was held in Italy in 1990. Now it was under the firmest of scrutiny with every decision made by the officials viewed as suspicious at first glance. The decision made by the FIGC to award Inter Milan the league title (known as the *Scudetto*) for the 2005/06 season was widely criticised and further damaged the reputation of the game, contributing to the decline of football in Italy both on the pitch and on the terraces. A study carried out by Demos & Pi (a polling company) in 2011 showed that the number of Italians who identified themselves as supporters of clubs in Italy had dropped from 52 per cent to 45 per cent. Moreover, 55 per cent of them said they were suspicious whenever an official made a mistake during a game.

The results for the national team were mixed during the latter half of 2006 after they became World Champions. None of the starting 11 in Berlin were in the team when Italy played Croatia at Stadio Armando Picchi in Livorno on 16 August in front of a crowd of just over 16,000. Croatia won the match 2-0. Given the complete team change made by Roberto Donadoni and the fallout from the recent scandal, the result was not entirely unbelievable.

What did fit into this category occurred in the next match which took place on 2 September. The game against Lithuania was played in Naples in front of 60,000 fans and was the Azzurri's first competitive match since being crowned World Champions. The team selection was far more recognisable this time around and it was Italy's first match in the qualifying group (B) for the upcoming 2008 Euros. The match finished all-square at 1-1 and it was back to losing ways just four days later when France gained revenge for the World Cup win, with a 3-1 victory on home soil in the qualifying group.

Italy finished the year with two wins in the group (against Ukraine and Georgia) before drawing against Turkey in Bergamo.

For the next ten years, Italy qualified for all the major competitions that they entered. This consisted of three European Championships and two World Cups. Italy's placings in all three of the UEFA-based competitions were pretty solid too. They went out at the quarter-final stage in 2008 (Switzerland/Austria) and 2016 (France), losing out on penalties to Spain (eventual winners) and Germany, respectively. They were finalists in 2012 (Poland/Ukraine), but the manner of defeat in the final against Spain was a significant one for the Azzurri. Spain had enjoyed 52 per cent of the possession, both teams had five attempted shots off target with Spain having nine shots on target and Italy six, so statistically, the final was a close affair – but the reality was that Spain were clinical and ripped apart the Italian rearguard to score the all-important four goals that gave them a comprehensive victory. Not since the World Cup defeat in 1970 against Brazil, had Italy been torn apart in a final. They had lost on penalties to Brazil in the 1994 World Cup and sudden death in the 2000 European Championship against the French, and had gone pound-for-pound with their opponents, but this was very different.

Perhaps the clearest indication of what would take place later came in the two World Cup campaigns in that time period. Italy failed to get past the group stages in 2010 (South Africa) and 2014 (Brazil). Their only victory came against England in 2014. In 2010, they finished bottom of the group with Paraguay, Slovakia and New Zealand all above the World Champions.

Despite the relegation and points deduction, Juventus won Serie B in the 2006/07 season, amassing 85 points, which was six more than Napoli and seven more than Genoa, who were also promoted. The following seasons, back in Serie A, were based on stability for the team from Turin, finishing third and second before consecutive seventh-place finishes. In the 2011/12 season they were once again crowned champions of Italy, a title that they held for the following eight seasons.

It was not just the *Calciopoli* scandal which caused problems for Italian football. There has also been an issue with the clubs' infrastructure.

Back in 1990, when Italy hosted the World Cup, there is no doubt that whilst the team faced semi-final heartbreak at the hands of Argentina, the tournament itself was a spectacular success. From the moment that Italy were awarded the finals a few years before, the work undertaken by the government and the local municipalities brought about significant investment in improving existing stadium infrastructures and building new ones as well. Those which benefited from renovation included San Paolo in Naples, Stadio Olimpico in Rome, San Siro in Milan, Stadio Comunale in Florence and the Luigi Ferraris in Genoa. Conversely, Italian fans could marvel at the new designs that were built, such as Stadio San Nicola in Bari, and the Delle Alpi in Turin. Running tracks were included in the new stadiums to allow other sports to benefit as well. The estimated cost was believed to be in the region of one billion lire, which significantly exceeded any original costings made.

Italian stadiums had, by and large, been built many decades before the finals by the local municipalities, and were thus not owned by the clubs themselves. This model had served Italian clubs well, as it allowed them to concentrate more on overseas player acquisitions and as a result, Diego Maradona graced the football pitches at Napoli and across the country. The same can be said of Michel Platini, who starred for his native France as they won the 1984 European Championship whilst plying his domestic trade with Juventus. A few years later and it would be AC Milan who were able to capture three of the greatest Dutch players of their generation who went on to lift the 1988 championship. These were Frank Rijkaard, Marco van Basten and Ruud Gullit. The final in 1990 was by no means a classic match when West Germany beat Argentina, but the victors boasted three key players who were employed by Inter Milan. These were Lothar Matthäus, Andreas Brehme and Jürgen Klinsmann. A year after the finals and it was two of the main stars

213

for England who arrived in Italy to play their domestic football, in the shape of Paul Gascoigne and David Platt.

Italy and the football played there was *'de rigueur'*. Aston Villa of England were drawn to play Inter Milan in the second round of the UEFA Cup in the latter stages of 1990. European games against teams from other nations were greeted with fever pitch excitement (especially with it being the first year that English clubs were allowed back into European competitions), but nothing compared to being drawn against an Italian side at that time.

There is no doubt that the golden decades of Italian football both on the pitch and in terms of the stadiums themselves were the 1980s and 1990s. Italian football walked tall and acted fine. However, there was a wind of change that soon altered the football landscape and the way in which the fans would experience it.

The original stadium designs (not only in Italy) were based on quantity and not necessarily quality, with the emphasis on getting as many fans in them as possible. This was done to the detriment of fan comfort, but in fairness allowed for a passionate atmosphere that fostered a sense of community. At the turn of the 21st century, stadium design introduced a more sophisticated and aesthetically pleasing experience for fans. One of the first European clubs to make such a change was Bayern Munich and the Allianz Arena, with its stunning light display. Technology also played a pivotal role in development of grounds with state-of-the-art facilities that included giant LED screens and wireless connectivity to provide the fan with truly immersive experiences that continued outside of the stadiums as well as inside. A key phase that followed for stadium architecture was to develop a growing emphasis on sustainability, with eco-friendly elements introduced, such as green roofs and solar panels in order to reduce environmental impact and make them as energy efficient as possible. However, the most recent and compelling changes centre around venues being built for multifunctional usage, incorporating not only football, but other major sports such as NFL, concerts, conferences, fan zones, executive boxes, hotels, shops, and leisure, thus making them attractive for all-year purpose.

In relation to all this progress, the first issue facing Italian football was one of timing. The heavy investments made for Italia 90 had come a few years before the revolution started to take shape. Additionally, very few clubs in Italy own their stadiums. As previously stated, they are owned by local municipalities. Invariably this has led to intense bureaucracy and difficulty in obtaining the financial resources to renovate or build new grounds. Red tape has historically impacted regulations, in particular pertaining to safety, which has affected capacity, although it is important to note that fan safety has always been paramount in any decisions made. Another issue facing local authorities was one of financial constraint, with many of them experiencing a severe economic downturn over a number of years, which has affected the carrying-out of improvements required for domestic use, let alone international purposes. Another factor is the historical and cultural significance of some of the stadiums, which makes it nigh on impossible to tear them down and rebuild. There are exceptions and one, most notably (and least surprisingly), relates to Juventus. Their new stadium was opened in 2011 and has invigorated the team from Turin and their fans, who are now able to spend additional money on merchandise and other services. The stadium boasts new restaurants, a shopping mall and a museum for people from all over the world to find out so much more about the club's history and where they are going. It also boasts modern executive features and when it was opened in 2011 the (then) chairman Giovanni Cobolli Gigli described the stadium as 'a source of great pride'.

It became only the fourth stadium in Italy to reach UEFA Category 4 level, which relates to the highest technical aspects in stadium infrastructure regulations. The other three are the San Siro, the Stadio Olimpico di Roma, and the Stadio Olimpico Grande Torino. Juventus bought the stadium from the local council in 2002 and with it, bought immediate approval from their fan base. The old one had a capacity of 67,000 but on average was only up to two thirds full. The decision to give the new stadium a capacity of just 41,000 has been a salient one for the Turin giants. Since its inception, it has hosted several finals for both the men's and women's game. One of the key aspects of modern football stadium design is to make sure that it is used for more than just the 19 domestic games (plus cup matches) in a season.

Juventus have made this possible themselves and remain the blueprint for others to follow if they are able to.

The decline of stadiums, lack of seats, violence and racism in recent years have led to many fans simply preferring to watch matches from the comfort of their own homes. Inevitably, this has led to a significant decline in matchday attendances and the knock-on effect for clubs has seen a decline in matchday revenues. However, the silver lining for clubs has been increased broadcasting rights, which has counteracted that somewhat.

From the 1982/83 season to the 1997/98 campaign, Italy dominated representation in the final of Europe's most prestigious club competition. Victory may not have been claimed in all of the finals, but it is still a remarkable achievement that an Italian club contested 12 out of a possible 16.

It wasn't just about team success either. On a similar timeline, the Ballon d'Or was won 13 times by players who represented Italian clubs. Firstly, it was Paolo Rossi in 1982 and Michel Platini in 1983, 1984 and 1985. Both of them were playing for Juventus at the time they were crowned the best player in the world. They were soon joined by Ruud Gullit in 1987, followed by fellow Dutchman Marco van Basten in 1988 and 1989. This time, AC Milan were the proud club that both players represented. It was the turn of Inter Milan in 1990 when Lothar Matthäus won the award. AC Milan's Van Basten was the winner once more in 1992 (to make his tally three). The following year saw Juventus's Roberto

Baggio crowned as the best player. The other winners in a glorious time for Italian football in the nineties were George Weah of AC Milan (1995), Ronaldo of Inter Milan (1997) and the mercurial Zinedine Zidane, who represented Juventus in the following year.

European Cup/Champions League finals

Season	Winners	Runners-up	Venue and Attendance
1982/83	Hamburg	Juventus	Olympic Stadium, Athens, Greece 73,500
1983/84	Liverpool	Roma	Stadio Olimpico, Rome, Italy 69,693
1984/85	Juventus	Liverpool	Heysel Stadium, Brussels, Belgium 58,000
1985/86	Steaua București	Barcelona	Ramón Sánchez Pizjuán, Seville, Spain 70,000
1986/87	Porto	Bayern Munich	Praterstadion, Vienna, Austria 57,500
1987/88	PSV Eindhoven	Benfica	Neckarstadion, Stuttgart, West Germany 68,000
1988/89	Milan	Steaua București	Camp Nou, Barcelona, Spain 97,000
1989/90	Milan	Benfica	Praterstadion, Vienna, Austria 57,558
1990/91	Red Star Belgrade	Marseille	Stadio San Nicola, Bari, Italy 56,000
1991/92	Barcelona	Sampdoria	Wembley Stadium, London, England 70,827
1992/93	Marseille	Milan	Olympiastadion, Munich, Germany 64,400
1993/94	Milan	Barcelona	Olympic Stadium, Athens, Greece 70,000
1994/95	Ajax	Milan	Ernst-Happel-Stadion, Vienna, Austria 49,730
1995/96	Juventus	Ajax	Stadio Olimpico, Rome, Italy 70,000
1996/97	Borussia Dortmund	Juventus	Olympiastadion, Munich, Germany 59,000
1997/98	Real Madrid	Juventus	Amsterdam Arena, Amsterdam, Netherlands 48,500

Since then (up to the 2023/24 season), Italian clubs have appeared in only six finals (although it is important to note that both AC Milan and Juventus contested the 2002/03 final). The three victories recorded during this period were AC Milan (2002/03 and 2006/07) and Inter Milan (2009/10). The only other victories in any European competition since 2010 came from Roma, who won the inaugural European Conference League in the 2021/22 season, and Atalanta, who claimed victory in the 2023/24 Europa League.

The recent wins have been warmly welcomed, but the lack of trophies in Europe's premier competition (or even representation in the final) tells the stark story that Italy have not been the threat that they once were in Europe for many years now. Serie A has long since been overtaken as the best league in the region with England, Germany, Spain and France holding court and becoming the places where the best footballers ply their trade week in and week out.

Italy's coefficiency has taken severe knocks over the past decade or so, when they have been rated as the fourth best league in Europe – a million miles away from when they held top spot for many years previously.

Since 2006, when Italy were crowned World Champions, there have been eight different managers of the national team, averaging out to just over two seasons per manager (or one qualifying campaign). In contrast, Germany have employed three as have the French, and England have announced contracts for five permanent managers over the period.

Between 1977 and 2004 (when Marcello Lippi was made manager for the first time), Italy employed just six managers. Where once there had been continuity and stability, there was now a regular changing of the guard, which proved to be a complete antithesis to what had gone before. With these changes came different ideologies and strategies.

During the victorious 2006 World Cup campaign, Lippi was widely acknowledged and indeed praised for being able to adapt game by game and use several key tactical set-ups that were designed to accommodate the team's playmakers, notably Andrea Pirlo and Francesco Totti. The most effective system was a 4-2-3-1 formation where Totti played in a more offensive role that complemented the defensive role for Pirlo. This worked perfectly during the latter stages of the competition, with Italy being able to call on attacking full-backs with effective wingers and box-to-box midfield players. Lippi's managerial skills, which were highlighted in 2006, included his tactical prowess, coaching skills and his ability to motivate his players.

When he was in his second spell as the leader of the national team, things had changed somewhat and some of Lippi's decisions were put under scrutiny, including his selection for the 2010 campaign in South Africa, when he left out some of Italy's exciting new breed, such as Mario Balotelli.

Cesare Prandelli was in charge when Italy reached the final of the European Championship in 2012. The formation deployed by Prandelli was likened to how Spain played at that time which relied heavily on short passing and ball retention moving through the various channels, more commonly known as *'tiki-taka'*. The system that Italy played during the group stages was based on a 3-5-2 formation which was changed to a standard 4-4-2 in the knockout stages. This proved to be an effective way of playing for Prandelli, but in the final his team was dismantled by the Spaniards who were the true masters of *'tiki-taka'*, and Italy lost the match 4-0.

It was once more against Spain that another manager's tactics came in question. This time it happened during the 2018 World Cup qualifying campaign. Italy and Spain were neck-and-neck going into a crucial match in Spain in September of 2017 with both nations on 16 points. Gian Piero Ventura was the man in charge and for this match he played a 4-2-4 formation. The tactics were a disaster, with Spain dominating play, winning the game 3-0. Ventura was much criticised for this decision and would not last much longer in the hot seat. During his tenure, the players held emergency meetings without the manager in attendance. The Italian public were often dismayed by the lack of variation in the way that Ventura got his team to play. Against Sweden in the play-offs, he used a system that had three centre-backs in operation but it was a totally redundant tactic given Sweden were camped deep in their own half, easily managing to deal with anything that came into their penalty area either in the air or on the ground.

The classic Italian style of play from many successful decades before had been based on good defence and retaining possession. More recently, the defences have been by-and-large not as effective as those that came before them. The possession base and hitting other teams at critical times has diminished over time as well.

The decision to appoint Roberto Mancini proved to be a master stroke and turned the tide for the Azzurri, winning the European Championship in 2021. The country was united once more. Mancini's preferred style was based on a 4-3-3 formation with which his team developed a winning mentality based on offensive football where possession was key. His teams broke records and the hearts of the English in 2021 at Wembley, their home soil. Mancini blended players of different ages, giving youth the chance to shine alongside the more mature.

Just a few days before the start of the 2024 Euro finals, the BBC reported on whether Italy were ready to defend the competition. The column (written by Mina Rzouki) recalled the scenes of a great Italian night in London in the summer of 2001:

'The enduring image of Roberto Mancini and Gianluca Vialli embracing as Italy celebrated victory at Wembley Stadium on 11 July 2021 will forever be etched in the minds of the nation. It was the culmination of an extraordinary project designed to set the national team on a new path.'

The column then went on to look at Italy three years later in the summer of 2024, centring around the image previously spoken about. Vialli had sadly succumbed to pancreatic cancer and Mancini was no longer at the helm after five years in the job. Luciano Spalletti was now the man tasked with bringing back glory after leading Napoli back to the summit of Serie A. A feat that had been 33 years in the making.

The article then went on to gauge the views of one of Italy's finest club managers, Carlo Ancelotti, who served up some stark messages ahead of the finals:

'I don't see top-class players [in the Italy squad] except Donnarumma, in goal. At Euro 2020, Italy could count on the revered and serial-winning defensive duo of Giorgio Chiellini and Leonardo Bonucci. In the middle they boasted the creativity of Marco Verratti, while up front they had the technique and genius of Lorenzo Insigne and Domenico Berardi. None of those players will be in Germany and nor will be their most experienced defender, Inter's Francesco Acerbi, who had to pull out after picking up an injury. Instead, Italy will be relying on several new faces to prove their worth and the power of one superstar coach, Spalletti. Famous for being one of Italy's finest tacticians, Spalletti was always complimented for his teams' style of play but criticised for his inability to win trophies. Winning the Scudetto with Napoli while playing the most captivating brand of football in Europe finally earned him the respect he deserved. Under his guidance, individuals always shine, while the patterns of play have often proved tantalising. The problem is, he has not had much time at the helm of this Azzurri side to design the perfect set-up that would extract the quality of these younger individuals.'

The article then went on to discuss tactics that had been deployed by Spalletti. During the qualifying campaign, the Italian manager's starting position tactically was based on a 4-3-3 formation. However, this hadn't been the case in friendly matches where it was not unusual to play three at the back. This led to cries of too many instructions for the team with the players looking vulnerable to the counter-attack.

The report concluded that:

'It may not be a squad comparable to those of the past, which brimmed with quality all over the pitch, but Italy seem certain they possess a united, hard-working team that will fight for the result. One should never underestimate the Azzurri, but the question is, are Italy actually ready for this tournament?'

The need to pit their tactical wits against some of the greatest nations to ever play the game is just one obstacle the Italian national management has had to face. The other major one has been the club versus country debate. If the country was united in 2021 after the Euros success, then the rifts started to appear once more just a few short months later as Italy failed to qualify for their second successive World Cup. This was felt most acutely in the play-offs, in which Italy lost to North Macedonia.

To assist in the build-up to the match, the Italian Football Federation had made a request for Serie A to amend its calendar and move league matches from the weekend before the crucial match, thus allowing for Roberto Mancini to spend more time with his players in preparation. However, the request was turned down, much to the dismay of Mancini and the federation. The impact of the decision and the subsequent defeat was not lost on federation president, Gabriele Gravina, who stated, 'There is always great resistance from the clubs towards the national team.' Gravina added comments that summed up the situation well but were somewhat alarming at the same time: 'The national team is seen more as an annoyance than something that unites an entire country.'

On the eve of the 2022 World Cup, it was reported that state broadcaster RAI refused to move a friendly match against Austria to the night before (so there was no clash with the opening match of the tournament) as they preferred to air a popular light entertainment programme, *Dancing with the Stars*. When asked in an interview what was a major cause, RAI national team analyst, Antonio Di Gennaro commented, 'Provincialism has been an issue and as far as players sometimes not wanting to go to the national team because of injury problems. Those are situations that regard the clubs.'

Italian striker Ciro Immobile was stopped from boarding a plane by his club (Lazio) as he attempted to join his fellow countrymen for a Nations League clash in Hungary. The reason cited was an injury. Often, Italian clubs will stand firm when it comes to their most treasured assets playing for the national team, with risk aversion paramount. This has led to the Azzurri being seen as an afterthought and at times, a major inconvenience to the domestic game which rules the country. The Italian national team suffers from not having the identity that has been afforded to the domestic game. A prime example of this has been that for matches on home soil, the national team travels the country and only plays the biggest matches at grounds such as the San Siro in Milan or the Stadio Olimpico in Rome.

Regardless of any issues with clubs or the media sector, in some ways the national team has only got itself to blame for its failures. There have been pivotal moments in qualifying matches when they simply have not been able to take advantage of situations presented to them. This was no more pertinent than in the 2022 qualifying campaign and the games played against Switzerland, with penalties missed by Jorginho in both matches, which ended in draws. Conversions would have meant that the need to contest the play-offs would have been a redundant one for Italy and it would have been the Swiss playing in them and having the restless nights instead. The magnitude of those penalty misses was not lost on Jorginho either: 'Stepping up there twice and not being able to help your team and your country is something that I will carry with me forever. People say we need to lift our heads and carry on, but it is tough.'

There are other variables. What if Spinazzola had been available for matches instead of sitting them out? Then there was Alessandro Florenzi against Bulgaria; Beradi missing chances that were perhaps easier to score against North Macedonia. There are plenty of 'what-if' moments to pontificate on. And many have done just that.

Notwithstanding the achievements in 2021, the decline of Italian football has been in evidence since it reached the dizzy heights of 2006. There are two main reasons for this: lack of talent and succession planning at the highest levels of the game.

One of the main issues in the 2018 qualifying campaign was that Italy were essentially dining out on past achievements and reputations, and changes were not made quickly enough. The issue of having multiple managers would not have done anything positive to change the status quo. Complacency was the rot that had set in. Italy had been guilty of looking backwards as opposed to forwards.

A major reason why Italy didn't qualify for the 2022 finals centred on player development. Over the years, there has been an alarming decline in the number of players who can step up to the international stage in the same way they had in the latter part of the 20th century and indeed at the start of the new millennium. A salient point is that veteran players were thought of more highly than the younger talents coming through. In the past decade, players such as Lorenzo Insigne, Ciro Immobile, Alessio Romagnoli, Giacomo Bonaventura and Jorginho have been ignored (amongst others) without any satisfactory reason given.

The Italian Football Federation promised to make changes that would help. Carlo Tavecchio was appointed president of the Federation on 11 August 2014 (and later re-elected). He pledged to follow the German model by opening national football centres all across the country. The projected target was 200 but initially just 30 opened. His other pledge was to reduce the number of teams in Serie A from 20 to 18, reversing the decision from 2004. To date, in 2024, there are still 20 teams participating in Italy's premier league.

Italy have not been able to hold on to their younger players in the last decade or so. The team that reached the final of the Under-21 European Championship in Israel in 2013 featured the likes of Ciro Immobile, Luca Caldirola and Giulio Donati. All of these players were playing their domestic football in Germany just a couple of years later. Marco Verratti played an important part in the championship but found himself at Paris Saint Germain soon after. Italy's final appearance in 2013 (they lost to Spain) has been their last one to date, whereas from

1992 to 2004, Italy won the competition five times. This in itself highlights the alarming decline from the levels that meant Italy had once been held in the highest esteem in not only European football, but in the world.

These stats are concerning to any fan of Italian football, but the issue they face is that players have not been nurtured in the way that they have been in Germany, England, Spain and France. The larger clubs have been guilty of not actually trusting the process to take the time to bring their younger and most valuable assets through, and in many cases, these players have not wanted to go back to their parent clubs when they have been loaned out.

Another issue that Italy has faced is one of diversity. Over the years, a number of European nations have become more diverse in their demographics. This has brought success to the likes of France and to a lesser degree, England. Immigration has played a major part in this, but Italy does not have the same demographic and immigration process.

This is illustrated by the French team that were victorious in the 1998 World Cup held on home soil. An article written by Nils Adler for *Aljazeera* on 30 November 2022 contained salient points on how immigration aided the French national team:

'The team, typically known as Les Bleus but nicknamed this time "Black, Blanc, Beur" (Black, White and Arab) in the media during the 1998 tournament, was hailed as a shining example of successful integration. French newspaper *Le Monde* labelled them a "symbol of the diversity and of the unity of the country". Then, French President Jacques Chirac described them as a "tricolour and multicolour team" that had created a "beautiful image of France and its humanity".'

Adler explained that France won the European Championship in 2020, with Zinedine Zidane named player of the tournament, and he then went on to highlight players who have been part of the French arsenal in more recent times:

'After narrowly losing the 2016 European Championship final to Portugal, France would win the World Cup again in 2018.

'Just as it had been 20 years earlier, the France squad was a melting pot of different ethnicities, with 17 of the 23 players eligible to play for at least one other country.

'Among them was Kylian Mbappé, who has a father from Cameroon and a mother from Algeria and was voted the best young player of the tournament. Another standout player was Paul Pogba, a Muslim with Guinean parents, who, like Mbappé and many other players in the team, had grown up in the suburbs of Paris.'

Another article written by Laurence Connell for *Italy Magazine* on 6 September 2004 challenges the reason why Italy has not followed suit with the headline: 'Italy is Increasingly Multicultural. So Why Isn't its National Soccer Team?'

The centrepeice of the article related to the 2023 national first team debut of Destiny Udogie, who described the feeling as a 'dream come true'. Udogie was of African descent and became the newest member of a small group of black players that had represented Italy in the last few decades. The most high-profile of the group was Mario Balotelli, a decade before. Balotelli had not been the first but was a trailblazer in the sense that he represented his country on a regular basis.

The amount of money spent on youth structures has been nowhere near as high as in other countries, who have overtaken Italy pertaining to Europe's coefficiency requirements. UEFA coefficients are statistics based in weighted arithmetic means used for ranking and seeding teams in club and international competitions.

With serious investments being made in other countries such as Spain, England, Germany and others, Serie A has been helped by government intervention and a policy known as the Growth Decree, but this has now been halted, threatening Serie A once more. Emmet Gates wrote a report for *Forbes* that was published on 29 December 2023 with the headline: 'Serie A's Diminishing Global Appeal Takes Another Hit Amid Decree Axe'. The column went on to add:

'Never let it be said that Italy doesn't know how to sabotage its national sport. For years, various Italian governments and political parties have put up roadblocks when it comes to building new stadiums throughout the country, to the point where it has almost turned into a tragicomedy to see what kind of excuse politicians come up with in order to avoid erecting new arenas and modernise the Italian game. While clubs can be accused of lacking foresight down the years, namely in squandering TV money on players and coaches rather than infrastructure and a united vision on how to market Serie A and its product, the Italian state is now wandering down the same path.'

The article discusses the implications of scrapping the scheme which helped Italian football to go some way to compete with similar leagues in England, Germany and Spain. Its modus operandi was to entice the best talent to Italy. Not only in terms of football but other sports and skilled professionals. In the 21st century, Serie A teams have been able to bring in such esteemed talent as Cristiano Ronaldo, Romelu Lukaku and many others. In its purest form, the Decree was a tax relief for clubs to bring in such players.

The report added some financial stats and more reasons for clubs to worry further:

'According to website Calcio e Finanza, Roma have saved around $23m (€21m) in wages this season by using the Decree. Milan saved around $22m (€20m) and part of their ability to tie down star man Rafael Leão to a long-term contract was due to using the Decree. Juve saved around $18m (€17m), while Napoli $15m (€14m).'

Epilogue

I WAS drawn to the articles written about the Italian national team and how they would fare in the summer of 2024, following the Italian government's decision to remove the Growth Decree at the start of the year.

Mina Rzouki's work for the BBC recalled the memory and the beauty of Mancini and Vialli celebrating in unison at Wembley Stadium in 2021. The report outlined the thought process proffered by Carlo Ancelotti when stating that the only truly world-class player in the current Italian locker was Gianluigi Donnarumma. One simply cannot disagree with Ancelotti on this most moot of points. The question posed by Rzouki at the end of the article is that whilst the Azzurri can never be underestimated, were they ready for the Euros in 2024?

Having exited the tournament in the round of 16 at the hands of Switzerland, the obvious answer is that Italy were not ready. One only has to look at that game to understand why. Italy were second best in every department. The reality is that they struggled to qualify from the group stages as well. For long periods of the final game against Croatia, Italy looked like they would need to qualify as one of those best third-place finishers, and so would have to hope for the best in the remaining games in other groups. The last-gasp (but brilliant) equalising goal scored by Mattia Zaccagni ensured that his country would finish in second place.

The nuances of Italian football are formidable, with football, politics, regionalism and culture mixing and clashing on a daily basis. Add in apathy, an overconfidence, and the inability to make changes at important times, and Italian waters are seldom calm ones.

At first glance, the decision to stop the Growth Decree was bad for the Italian domestic game and ultimately, its national identity as well. Serie A can no longer attract overseas players with its attractive tax breaks and financial remuneration. However, this represents hope at the same time. Will those who reside in the Italian powerhouses and marbled halls finally have to recognise that changes need to be made? Surely this is the time to nurture their own talent and make the changes that are necessary to move the game in Italy forward. There is a long way to go, of that there is no doubt. Data and innovation will have to play their part and overseas investments need to be very attractive to those ready to dig deep.

Only time will tell if it works out well.

These final thoughts in the book were compiled just a few days after Italy boarded the plane to make the short journey back from Germany. After the next tranche of Nations League matches, just over the horizon is the qualifying competition for the 2026 World Cup, which is being held in the USA, Mexico and Canada. Whether Luciano Spalletti is the man to take Italy forward is a matter the Italian Football Federation must ponder. Spalletti has a contract that takes him up to 2026. Regardless of who is in charge, a third finals without Italy would be unthinkable.

#Italiafuoridaimondiali is something that needs to be consigned to the dustbin of history.

The Winning Squads:
FIFA World Cup

1934

No.	Pos.	Player	Date of birth (age)	Club
	DF	Luigi Allemandi	18 Nov 1903 (aged 30)	Ambrosiana-Inter
	FW	Pietro Arcari	2 Dec 1909 (aged 24)	Milan
	MF	Luigi Bertolini	13 Sep 1904 (aged 29)	Juventus
	FW	Felice Borel	5 April 1914 (aged 20)	Juventus
	DF	Umberto Caligaris	26 July 1901 (aged 32)	Juventus
	MF	Armando Castellazzi	7 Sep 1904 (aged 29)	Ambrosiana-Inter
	GK	Giuseppe Cavanna	18 Sep 1905 (aged 28)	Napoli
	GK	Gianpiero Combi (c)	20 Nov 1902 (aged 31)	Juventus
	FW	Attilio Demaria	19 March 1909 (aged 25)	Ambrosiana-Inter
	FW	Giovanni Ferrari	6 Dec 1907 (aged 26)	Juventus
	MF	Attilio Ferraris	26 March 1904 (aged 30)	Roma
	FW	Enrique Guaita	11 July 1910 (aged 23)	Roma
	FW	Anfilogino Guarisi	26 Dec 1905 (aged 28)	Lazio
	GK	Guido Masetti	22 Nov 1907 (aged 26)	Roma
	MF	Giuseppe Meazza	23 Aug 1910 (aged 23)	Ambrosiana-Inter
	MF	Luis Monti	15 May 1901 (aged 33)	Juventus
	DF	Eraldo Monzeglio	5 June 1906 (aged 27)	Bologna
	FW	Raimundo Orsi	2 Dec 1901 (aged 32)	Juventus
	MF	Mario Pizziolo	7 Dec 1909 (aged 24)	Fiorentina
	DF	Virginio Rosetta	25 Feb 1902 (aged 32)	Juventus
	FW	Angelo Schiavio	15 Sep 1905 (aged 28)	Bologna
	MF	Mario Varglien	26 Dec 1905 (aged 28)	Juventus

1938

No.	Pos.	Player	Date of birth (age)	Club
	MF	Michele Andreolo	6 Sep 1912 (aged 25)	Bologna
	FW	Sergio Bertoni	23 Sep 1915 (aged 22)	Pisa

FW	Amedeo Biavati	4 April 1915 (aged 23)	Bologna
GK	Carlo Ceresoli	14 May 1910 (aged 28)	Bologna
MF	Bruno Chizzo	19 April 1916 (aged 22)	Triestina
FW	Gino Colaussi	4 March 1914 (aged 24)	Triestina
MF	Aldo Donati	29 Sep 1910 (aged 27)	Roma
FW	Giovanni Ferrari	6 Dec 1907 (aged 30)	Ambrosiana-Inter
FW	Pietro Ferraris	15 Feb 1912 (aged 26)	Ambrosiana-Inter
DF	Alfredo Foni	20 Jan 1911 (aged 27)	Juventus
MF	Mario Genta	1 March 1912 (aged 26)	Genoa
MF	Ugo Locatelli	5 Feb 1916 (aged 22)	Ambrosiana-Inter
GK	Guido Masetti	22 Nov 1907 (aged 30)	Roma
MF	Giuseppe Meazza (c)	23 Aug 1910 (aged 27)	Ambrosiana-Inter
DF	Eraldo Monzeglio	5 June 1906 (aged 31)	Roma
GK	Aldo Olivieri	2 Sep 1910 (aged 27)	Lucchese
MF	Renato Olmi	12 July 1914 (aged 23)	Ambrosiana-Inter
FW	Piero Pasinati	21 July 1910 (aged 27)	Triestina
MF	Mario Perazzolo	7 June 1911 (aged 26)	Genoa
FW	Silvio Piola	29 Sep 1913 (aged 24)	Lazio
DF	Pietro Rava	21 Jan 1916 (aged 22)	Juventus
MF	Pietro Serantoni	11 Dec 1906 (aged 31)	Roma

1982

No.	Pos.	Player	Date of birth (age)	Club
1	GK	Dino Zoff (c)	28 Feb 1942 (aged 40)	Juventus
2	DF	Franco Baresi	8 May 1960 (aged 22)	Milan
3	DF	Giuseppe Bergomi	22 Dec 1963 (aged 18)	Internazionale
4	DF	Antonio Cabrini	8 Sep 1957 (aged 24)	Juventus
5	DF	Fulvio Collovati	9 May 1957 (aged 25)	Milan
6	DF	Claudio Gentile	27 Sep 1953 (aged 28)	Juventus
7	DF	Gaetano Scirea	25 May 1953 (aged 29)	Juventus
8	DF	Pietro Vierchowod	6 April 1959 (aged 23)	Fiorentina
9	MF	Giancarlo Antognoni	1 April 1954 (aged 28)	Fiorentina
10	MF	Giuseppe Dossena	2 May 1958 (aged 24)	Torino
11	MF	Giampiero Marini	25 Feb 1951 (aged 31)	Internazionale
12	GK	Ivano Bordon	13 April 1951 (aged 31)	Internazionale
13	MF	Gabriele Oriali	25 Nov 1952 (aged 29)	Internazionale
14	MF	Marco Tardelli	24 Sep 1954 (aged 27)	Juventus
15	MF	Franco Causio	1 Feb 1949 (aged 33)	Udinese
16	MF	Bruno Conti	13 March 1955 (aged 27)	Roma
17	FW	Daniele Massaro	23 May 1961 (aged 21)	Fiorentina

18	FW	Alessandro Altobelli	28 Nov 1955 (aged 26)	Internazionale
19	FW	Francesco Graziani	16 Dec 1952 (aged 29)	Fiorentina
20	FW	Paolo Rossi	23 Sep 1956 (aged 25)	Juventus
21	FW	Franco Selvaggi	15 May 1953 (aged 29)	Cagliari
22	GK	Giovanni Galli	29 April 1958 (aged 24)	Fiorentina

2006

No.	Pos.	Player	Date of birth (age)	Club
1	GK	Gianluigi Buffon	28 Jan 1978 (aged 28)	Juventus
2	DF	Cristian Zaccardo	21 Dec 1981 (aged 24)	Palermo
3	DF	Fabio Grosso	28 Nov 1977 (aged 28)	Palermo
4	MF	Daniele De Rossi	24 July 1983 (aged 22)	Roma
5	DF	Fabio Cannavaro (c)	13 Sep 1973 (aged 32)	Juventus
6	DF	Andrea Barzagli	8 May 1981 (aged 25)	Palermo
7	FW	Alessandro Del Piero	9 Nov 1974 (aged 31)	Juventus
8	MF	Gennaro Gattuso	9 Jan 1978 (aged 28)	Milan
9	FW	Luca Toni	26 May 1977 (aged 29)	Fiorentina
10	FW	Francesco Totti	27 Sep 1976 (aged 29)	Roma
11	FW	Alberto Gilardino	5 July 1982 (aged 23)	Milan
12	GK	Angelo Peruzzi	16 Feb 1970 (aged 36)	Lazio
13	DF	Alessandro Nesta	19 March 1976 (aged 30)	Milan
14	GK	Marco Amelia	2 April 1982 (aged 24)	Livorno
15	FW	Vincenzo Iaquinta	21 Nov 1979 (aged 26)	Udinese
16	MF	Mauro Camoranesi	4 Sep 1976 (aged 29)	Juventus
17	MF	Simone Barone	30 April 1978 (aged 28)	Palermo
18	FW	Filippo Inzaghi	9 Aug 1973 (aged 32)	Milan
19	DF	Gianluca Zambrotta	19 Feb 1977 (aged 29)	Juventus
20	MF	Simone Perrotta	17 Sep 1977 (aged 28)	Roma
21	MF	Andrea Pirlo	19 May 1979 (aged 27)	Milan
22	DF	Massimo Oddo	14 June 1976 (aged 29)	Lazio
23	DF	Marco Materazzi	19 Aug 1973 (aged 32)	Internazionale

Key: DF = Defender, FW = Forward, MF = Midfielder, GK = Goalkeeper.

The Winning Squads: UEFA European Championship

1968

No.	Pos.	*Player*	*Date of birth (age)*	*Club*
1	GK	Enrico Albertosi	2 Nov 1939 (aged 28)	Fiorentina
2	FW	Pietro Anastasi	7 April 1948 (aged 20)	Varese
3	DF	Angelo Anquilletti	25 April 1943 (aged 25)	Milan
4	DF	Giancarlo Bercellino	9 Sep 1941 (aged 26)	Juventus
5	DF	Tarcisio Burgnich	25 April 1939 (aged 29)	Internazionale
6	FW	Giacomo Bulgarelli	24 Sep 1940 (aged 27)	Bologna
7	DF	Ernesto Castano	2 May 1939 (aged 29)	Juventus
8	MF	Giancarlo De Sisti	13 March 1943 (aged 25)	Fiorentina
9	FW	Angelo Domenghini	25 Aug 1941 (aged 26)	Internazionale
10	DF	Giacinto Facchetti (c)	18 July 1942 (aged 25)	Internazionale
11	MF	Giorgio Ferrini	18 Aug 1939 (aged 28)	Torino
12	MF	Aristide Guarneri	7 March 1938 (aged 30)	Bologna
13	MF	Antonio Juliano	26 Dec 1942 (aged 25)	Napoli
14	MF	Giovanni Lodetti	10 Aug 1942 (aged 25)	Milan
15	FW	Sandro Mazzola	8 Nov 1942 (aged 25)	Internazionale
16	FW	Pierino Prati	13 Dec 1946 (aged 21)	Milan
17	FW	Gigi Riva	7 Nov 1944 (aged 23)	Cagliari
18	MF	Gianni Rivera	18 Aug 1943 (aged 24)	Milan
19	DF	Roberto Rosato	18 Aug 1943 (aged 24)	Milan
20	DF	Sandro Salvadore	29 Nov 1939 (aged 28)	Juventus
21	GK	Lido Vieri	16 July 1939 (aged 28)	Torino
22	GK	Dino Zoff	28 Feb 1942 (aged 26)	Napoli

2020

No.	Pos.	Player	Date of birth (age)	Club
1	GK	Salvatore Sirigu	12 Jan 1987 (aged 34)	Torino
2	DF	Giovanni Di Lorenzo	4 Aug 1993 (aged 27)	Napoli
3	DF	Giorgio Chiellini (c)	14 Aug 1984 (aged 36)	Juventus
4	DF	Leonardo Spinazzola	25 March 1993 (aged 28)	Roma
5	MF	Manuel Locatelli	8 Jan 1998 (aged 23)	Sassuolo
6	MF	Marco Verratti	5 Nov 1992 (aged 28)	Paris St Germain
7	MF	Gaetano Castrovilli	17 Feb 1997 (aged 24)	Fiorentina
8	MF	Jorginho	20 Dec 1991 (aged 29)	Chelsea
9	FW	Andrea Belotti	20 Dec 1993 (aged 27)	Torino
10	FW	Lorenzo Insigne	4 June 1991 (aged 30)	Napoli
11	FW	Domenico Berardi	1 Aug 1994 (aged 26)	Sassuolo
12	MF	Matteo Pessina	21 April 1997 (aged 24)	Atalanta
13	DF	Emerson Palmieri	3 Aug 1994 (aged 26)	Chelsea
14	MF	Federico Chiesa	25 Sep 1997 (aged 23)	Juventus
15	DF	Francesco Acerbi	10 Feb 1988 (aged 33)	Lazio
16	MF	Bryan Cristante	3 March 1995 (aged 26)	Roma
17	FW	Ciro Immobile	20 Feb 1990 (aged 31)	Lazio
18	MF	Nicolò Barella	7 Feb 1997 (aged 24)	Internazionale
19	DF	Leonardo Bonucci	1 May 1987 (aged 34)	Juventus
20	MF	Federico Bernardeschi	16 Feb 1994 (aged 27)	Juventus
21	GK	Gianluigi Donnarumma	25 Feb 1999 (aged 22)	Milan
22	FW	Giacomo Raspadori	18 Feb 2000 (aged 21)	Sassuolo
23	DF	Alessandro Bastoni	13 April 1999 (aged 22)	Internazionale
24	DF	Alessandro Florenzi	11 March 1991 (aged 30)	Paris St Germain
25	DF	Rafael Tolói	10 Sep 1990 (aged 30)	Atalanta
26	GK	Alex Meret	22 March 1997 (aged 24)	Napoli

FIFA World Cup Record

Year	Round	Pld	W	D*	L	GF	GA
Uruguay 1930	Did not enter						
Italy 1934	Champions	5	4	1	0	12	3
France 1938	Champions	4	4	0	0	11	5
Brazil 1950	Group stage	2	1	0	1	4	3
Switzerland 1954	Group stage	3	1	0	2	6	7
Sweden 1958	Did not qualify						
Chile 1962	Group stage	3	1	1	1	3	2
England 1966	Group stage	3	1	0	2	2	2
Mexico 1970	Runners-up	6	3	2	1	10	8
West Germany 1974	Group stage	3	1	1	1	5	4
Argentina 1978	Fourth place	7	4	1	2	9	6
Spain 1982	Champions	7	4	3	0	12	6
Mexico 1986	Round of 16	4	1	2	1	5	6
Italy 1990	Third place	7	6	1	0	10	2
United States 1994	Runners-up	7	4	2	1	8	5
France 1998	Quarter-finals	5	3	2	0	8	3
South Korea/Japan 2002	Round of 16	4	1	1	2	5	5
Germany 2006	Champions	7	5	2	0	12	2
South Africa 2010	Group stage	3	0	2	1	4	5
Brazil 2014	Group stage	3	1	0	2	2	3
Russia 2018	Did not qualify						
Qatar 2022	Did not qualify						
Total	4 titles	83	45	21	17	128	77

*Denotes draws include knockout matches decided via penalty shoot-out.

Most appearances at the FIFA World Cup:
Paolo Maldini: 23
Most appearances in the FIFA World Cup qualifiers:
Gianluigi Buffon: 39
Most appearances at the FIFA World Cup and in FIFA World Cup qualifiers:
Fabio Cannavaro: 50
Most minutes played in FIFA World Cup matches:
Paolo Maldini: 2,216 minutes
Most FIFA World Cups as part of the squad
Gianluigi Buffon: 5 (1998, 2002, 2006, 2010, 2014)
Most FIFA World Cups played in:
Gianluigi Buffon, Gianni Rivera, Giuseppe Bergomi, Paolo Maldini and Fabio Cannavaro: 4 each
Most goals at the FIFA World Cup:
Christian Vieri, Paolo Rossi and Roberto Baggio: 9 each
Most goals at a single FIFA World Cup:
Paolo Rossi (1982) and Salvatore Schillaci (1990): 6 each
Most goals at the FIFA World Cup and in FIFA World Cup qualifiers:
Gigi Riva: 17
Most FIFA World Cups scored in:
Roberto Baggio: 3 (1990, 1994 and 1998)
Most goals in FIFA World Cup qualifiers:
Gigi Riva: 14
First goal in a FIFA World Cup match:
Angelo Schiavio: 27 May 1934, 7-1 vs United States
First goal in a FIFA World Cup qualifier:
Anfilogino Guarisi: 25 March 1934, 4-0 vs Greece
Most FIFA World Cups coached in:
Enzo Bearzot: 3
Most FIFA World Cup matches as a manager:
Enzo Bearzot: 18
Most FIFA World Cup matches won as a manager:
Enzo Bearzot: 9
Most FIFA World Cup titles as a manager:
Vittorio Pozzo: 2 (1934 and 1938)

UEFA European Championship Record

Year	Round	Pld	W	D*	L	GF	GA
France 1960	Did not enter						
Spain 1964	Did not qualify						
Italy 1968	Champions	3	1	2	0	3	1
Belgium 1972	Did not qualify						
Yugoslavia 1976	Did not qualify						
Italy 1980	Fourth place	4	1	3	0	2	1
France 1984	Did not qualify						
West Germany 1988	Semi-finals	4	2	1	1	4	3
Sweden 1992	Did not qualify						
England 1996	Group stage	3	1	1	1	3	3
Belgium/Netherlands 2000	Runners-up	6	4	1	1	9	4
Portugal 2004	Group stage	3	1	2	0	3	2
Austria/Switzerland 2008	Quarter-finals	4	1	2	1	3	4
Poland/Ukraine 2012	Runners-up	6	2	3	1	6	7
France 2016	Quarter-finals	5	3	1	1	6	2
Europe 2020	Champions	7	5	2	0	13	4
Germany 2024	Round of 16	4	1	1	2	3	5
Total	2 titles	49	22	19	8	55	36

*Denotes draws include knockout matches decided via penalty shoot-out.

Most appearances at the UEFA European Championship:
Leonardo Bonucci: 18
**Most appearances in UEFA European
Championship qualifying:**
Gianluigi Buffon: 41
**Most appearances at the UEFA European Championship and in
UEFA European Championship qualifying:**
Gianluigi Buffon: 58
Most minutes played in European Championship matches:
Leonardo Bonucci: 1,668 minutes
Most European Championships as part of the squad:
Alessandro Del Piero (1996, 2000, 2004, 2008), Gianluigi Buffon
(2004, 2008, 2012, 2016) and Giorgio Chiellini (2008, 2012,
2016, 2020): 4
Most UEFA European Championships played in:
Gianluigi Buffon, Alessandro Del Piero and Giorgio Chiellini: 4
Most goals at the UEFA European Championship:
Mario Balotelli and Antonio Cassano: 3 each
Most goals at a single UEFA European Championship:
Mario Balotelli (2012): 3
Most UEFA European Championships scored in:
Nicolò Barella (2020 and 2024), Leonardo Bonucci (2016 and
2020), Antonio Cassano (2004 and 2012), Andrea Pirlo (2008 and
2012): 2 each
**Most goals at the UEFA European Championship and in UEFA
European Championship qualifying:**
Filippo Inzaghi: 14
Most goals in UEFA European Championship qualifying:
Filippo Inzaghi: 12
First goal in a UEFA European Championship match:
Angelo Domenghini: 8 June 1968, 1-1 vs Yugoslavia
**First goal in a UEFA European Championship
qualifying match:**
Gianni Rivera: 2 Dec 1962, 6-0 vs. Turkey
Most UEFA European Championship matches as a manager:
Roberto Mancini: 7
**Most UEFA European Championship matches won
as a manager:**
Roberto Mancini: 5
Most UEFA European Championship titles as a manager:
Ferruccio Valcareggi (1968), Roberto Mancini (2020): 1

Acknowledgements

THERE WERE two blaring questions that I posed to myself prior to writing this book. The first was the obvious one. Just how did a country like Italy fail to reach consecutive finals? I hope that this has been addressed in previous chapters. The other conundrum was how do I compare this Italian situation with a Eurovision song that I loved (and still do) from some 50 years ago? Italian football (much likes its politics and other aspects of life) is all about the passion. It is also about drama, style and theatre, whilst maintaining substance – just like the song in question, that brought all this to my attention.

The Eurovision Song contest in 1974 will always be remembered for ABBA's 'Waterloo' entry for Sweden. It launched a phenomenal career for them which has lasted until today and no doubt, beyond as well. When people are asked their favourite song or moment from the competition, a significant number will reference ABBA.

This is not the case for me, although 'my' song does come from the same year, and was actually the runner-up to Waterloo. The song was called 'Si' and was performed by one of Italy's best-known entertainers,

Gigliola Cinquetti. Cinquetti was no stranger to the Eurovision Song Contest and had won it for Italy in 1964 with 'Non ho l'età' – translated as 'I'm not old enough (to love you)'. Cinquetti picked up a respectable 18 points for 'Si' (compared to ABBA's 24). 'Si' means 'yes' and the song courted controversy with politics, with the live telecast of the song in the competition being banned by the Italian national broadcaster RAI. At the same time as the contest, the Italian people were gearing up to vote in the 1974 Italian divorce referendum. Voters were asked whether they wanted to repeal a law passed just three years earlier, which had allowed divorce for the first time in modern Italy. Those voting 'yes' wanted to outlaw divorce once again, and those voting 'no' wanted to retain the law, which was still in its infancy. The song was thought to carry a political message (the term 'Si' was constantly used in it) and would curry favour and influence.

The song was in the first person and told the tale of a woman who admits to loving her partner and wants to spend the rest of her life with them. It is therefore a very positive song and, in the end, the 'No' voters won the referendum,1 obtaining nearly 60 per cent of the votes. It still remains one of the least known songs in Italy, despite its success in the competition and it really picked up traction in the UK when it was translated into English with the title 'Go (before you break my heart)'. This is how it first came to my attention and it reached the top ten in June 1974. The arrangement was identical to the

Italian version, but the lyrics and meaning profoundly changed the whole ethos of the song. It was still sung in the first person, but this time the lover wanted to leave the protagonist. Cinquetti acknowledges that the lover is sincere about the words that they are speaking. There is no way back for their relationship. She is telling them to go, before her heart completely breaks apart. She wishes to be alone with that heartbreak whilst sat deep in reflection. She knows that it will never be the same again.

It was that link that likened the first person in the song to the Italian nation in not reaching the World Cups in 2018 and 2022. Was it all a dream for the fervent Italian football lover? Would they wake up soon and just how would they face the lonely years without their love? Didn't the Italian national team know that the nation loves them so?

Listen to both versions of the song if you can: both sides of the 45 allowing the light and darkness to seep through the tear-stained curtains and on to the newly waxed floors.

As always, I would like to thank everyone at Pitch Publishing for making my dreams come true and allowing me to indulge myself with brilliant football matters that encompass the past, present and future. I have not finished. There are a thousand stories to be told.

Simon Goodyear has been my agent ever since I had my first book published. He will continue in this role because he is not only a fabulous representative but an equally brilliant person. Cheers, Si.

My family and friends have also provided their usual support and I love and thank them from the bottom of my heart. In particular, a big thanks to 'Our Emily' who worked hard on the fact-finding for me.

I would like to thank you for purchasing the book. I hope that you enjoyed reading it as much as I did writing it.

Finally, thank you Italy. I have been fascinated by the Azzurri ever since I watched them play England in the Bicentennial tournament in America in 1976 and also the qualifying group for the 1978 World Cup finals. It was Roberto Bettega that first caught my attention, followed by Paolo Rossi. The latter will always be known for his antics in 1982, but he was a major contributor to the 1978 team as well. Their victory in the 1982 final against West Germany was a momentous one, as were the matches against Argentina and Brazil earlier in the competition. The momentum carried through from the first qualifying round by Italy was on point. They will live long in my football memory.

I really believe that a tournament without the Italian team and its fan base is a poorer tournament. Just think of Italia 1990, USA 1994, Germany 2006, and several European Championship finals that Italy have competed in during the first quarter of the 21st century.

From the 'Divine Ponytail' in Roberto Baggio to the 'Berlin Wall' that was Fabio Cannavaro, Italy have had it all and will continue to greet victory and defeat in the same manner as they always have done.

The battle scars that are worn by the Italian players are always palpable ones, regardless of the result. They are always relevant, even at times when they are written off. And one must always tread carefully when it comes to writing off the Azzurri. Only the Italians themselves would have called the victory during the early stages of the competitions that they have gone on to win. This was most certainly the case in 1982, 2006 and 2021.

Has Marco Tardelli stopped running yet?

Bibliography

Books
Foot, J. *Calcio*: A History of Italian Football (Harper Perennial, 2007)

Websites
bbc.co.uk
theguardian.com
enfa.co.uk
theathletic.com
wikipedia.org
youtube.com
fourfourtwo.com
dailymail.co.uk
skysports.com
twitter.com
en-gb.facebook.com
mirror.co.uk
thetimes.co.uk
repubblica.it
usatoday.com
espn.com
meduim.com
apnews.com
forbes.com

Newspapers and Magazines
Corriere della Sera
La Repubblica
Italy Magazine
Aljazeera